LANDLORD SECRETS

LANDLORD SECRETS

A COMPLETE SYSTEM for MANAGING YOUR RENTAL PROPERTIES for MAXIMUM PROFIT!

MIKE LAUTENSACK

LIONCREST
PUBLISHING

LANDLORD SECRETS

A Complete System for Managing Your Rental Properties for Maximum Profit!

FIRST EDITION

ISBN 978-1-5445-4455-7 Hardcover
        978-1-5445-4453-3 Paperback
        978-1-5445-4454-0 Ebook

*I am grateful for the support and encouragement
I have received from my family on my professional journey.
Additionally, I could not have written this book
without the help of the Del Val team and
the opportunity to learn and grow
with such a fantastic company.*

CONTENTS

INTRODUCTION

"Ninety percent of all millionaires become so through owning real estate. More money has been made in real estate than in all industrial investments combined."

ANDREW CARNEGIE, Industrialist and Philanthropist

Carnegie's quote was written over one hundred years ago and is still as accurate today as it was then. For the average person, there are only a few avenues to wealth, and real estate investing continues to be the best way to achieve life-altering wealth.

Stocks and bonds offer a 5% to 10% return but have exceedingly high risk with no leverage or tax advantages. The bond market has been going up for thirty years, and stocks are at extraordinarily high levels. In fact, the S&P 500 was down over 18% in 2022, and bonds had their worst year ever. In my view these asset classes are unlikely to offer high returns over the next five to ten years.

There is gold, silver, and even bitcoin, but they all have high risk, no leverage, and no tax advantages.

You could start your own business, but you are looking at five to ten years of working long hours and assuming enormous risk. Over 90% of businesses fail in the first five years, and 90% of those that make it through the first five years fail within the next five years. Compare this to investing in residential real estate. The average returns for single-family or small multi-family investing have been in the 10% to 15% range over the last forty years.

Real estate investing offers many other advantages over these other asset classes. First, it provides a high degree of leverage. Most people can purchase an investment property with a 5% to 20% down payment and have the rest mortgaged. Try buying stocks, bonds, or bitcoin with that kind of leverage. Second, real estate has high tax advantages with depreciation and other costs being tax deductible. Third, real estate returns and cash flow are much less volatile than the other asset classes. Stocks can be up 30% one year and down 20% the next, as happened in 2022. Real estate investing is much smoother with less volatility in annual returns. Over the last forty years, real estate has only had negative returns during the "Great Recession" period of 2007 to 2010. To the average person, real estate investing is hands down the best vehicle for real wealth-building.

However, for real estate to produce a return, it must have tenants who pay rent. This is where it can become problematic. Most real estate investors are not great at managing their own properties because it is not the "sexy" part of real estate investing.

There are also many books and weekend courses on how to find and buy real estate, but not nearly as many on managing these properties once you own them. A recent Google search for the term "real estate investing" returned more than 9 million entries, whereas the term "property management for rental houses" returned only twenty-two thousand entries.

This book is here to help with this problem. *Landlord Secrets* will dramatically shorten the learning curve for new or small to midsized real estate investors managing their rental properties. It will also give the reader tips and tools to increase the profit and the value of their investment properties.

IS THIS BOOK RIGHT FOR YOU?

This book is not one of the thousands of others that teaches you how to buy and invest in real estate, nor is it for the large investors with hundreds, or even thousands, of units to manage. These folks likely have large staffs and professional systems in place.

Instead, this book is for individuals that are either thinking of becoming a real estate investor or currently own one, two, or a couple of dozen rental properties. They may be currently experiencing a problem and looking for advice on how to resolve it. They may also be looking for tools and tips to make their investments more profitable or have a high desire to become a more professional landlord.

This book is essentially arranged chronologically, beginning with getting your property ready for rent and finishing with accounting and taxes. As a result, reading from beginning to end is best but not required. If you need help in one particular area, there is nothing wrong with jumping to that section.

Being a landlord is not easy and it is not for everyone. It's primarily a people business. If you are not good at dealing with people, being a landlord may not be right for you. If that is the case, you might consider hiring a professional property manager (Chapter 15).

You may also be aware that landlords are on the list of hated or mocked professions along with attorneys and used-car salespeople. We need to raise the professional level of landlords. This can be done through education such as this book and national and local organizations promoting professional property management. I encourage all readers to join a national real estate investment club and a local chapter by going to the National Real Estate Investors Association: https://nationalreia.org/. Or even consider joining the National Association of Residential Property Managers (NARPM) by going to https://www.narpm.org/.

Being a landlord can be very rewarding. Knowing that you are helping people find homes where they may raise their families is an honorable goal. Landlords upgrade neighborhoods by taking properties that may have been neglected in the past and making needed improvements. Through this process they add value to the local area. Landlords contribute to the local economy by employing local vendors to maintain the property. They also pay taxes and bring money into local governments and economies. Landlords take risks like any business owner, but most give back to their local community and leave it a better place.

BECOMING A PROFESSIONAL LANDLORD

Being a professional landlord requires time and hard work. Many real estate investor gurus will tell you that it is easy to make money by renting properties, as if you just buy a rental property and start cashing checks. It does not work that way.

To make money, you must have tenants, some of which will present challenges. Some tenants may not pay the rent on time or at all. Tenants may damage the property and may not follow your rules and regulations. Using the tools and tips in this book will give you the upper hand in dealing with tenants and help you to avoid costly mistakes while maximizing your profits.

Most landlords will discover quickly that some tenants may try to bend the rules. A tenant may come to you and ask, "Would it be OK if I give you $500 today and pay the rest of the rent next week?" Or ask to use their security funds to cover this month's rent and they will "pay it back next month." These requests will seem genuine and often are, but how you respond to them will determine the success or failure of your rental business.

Like many things in business, having systems to rely on will make property management much easier. How and where do you collect rent? How are you going to respond to maintenance requests? Which software are you going to use? Which bookkeeping system are you going to use? These systems will make managing your properties much easier and, as a result, much more profitable.

The systems you are about to learn will help you:

- Fill vacancies faster
- Keep tenants longer
- Get higher rents than other landlords in the area
- Generate extra revenue with additional fees
- Avoid nonpayment issues
- Reduce maintenance costs
- Decide if you want to accept pets
- Enhance the sale value of your property
- Learn how to handle security deposits
- Perform tenant move-in and move-out inspections
- Utilize bookkeeping systems to track your income and expenses
- And much more

Your next question is likely, "OK, so I am interested in managing rental properties and learning these systems, but why should I listen to you on the subject?" That is a fair question.

MY ROAD AS A PROPERTY MANAGER

My name is Mike Lautensack and like many others (perhaps yourself included), I began my career in the corporate world but quickly became disenchanted with the long hours, high stress, travel, and constantly being away from my family.

I started real estate investing in 1999 to generate passive income and long-term wealth. Despite numerous mistakes and learning experiences, by 2006 I began to have some real success and made the leap to becoming a full-time real estate investor.

The following year, I founded the residential property management company known as Del Val Property Management LLC (Del Val), serving Philadelphia and the greater Delaware Valley outside Philadelphia. Today, Del Val is in its seventeenth year as a full-service residential property management company serving over 550 clients with over 5,000 single-family, multi-family, and HOA units under management. We have a staff of about thirty hardworking employees located in Malvern, Pennsylvania.

Since its inception seventeen years ago, Del Val has managed over 7,500 rental units, signed over 6,000 leases, and collected over $50 million in rent payments. We have had many successes but also many battles that have left scar tissue. These successes, as well as the scar tissue moments, have given me the expertise to write *Landlord Secrets*.

I have written hundreds of articles on property management, spoken at numerous industry events, participated in property management associations, and been a leader in the field for the last twenty years. But this book is the first time I have organized all this information into a complete landlord system.

My goal with this book is to be your real estate coach and help you avoid some of these scar tissue moments. This book will assist you in putting management systems in place that will make managing your tenants and rental properties much more straightforward and profitable.

GETTING STARTED

If you are ready to become a professional landlord and maximize the profits your rental properties generate, you have two choices: self-management or outsourced professional management.

SELF-MANAGEMENT

If you want to self-manage your own properties, this book is designed to help you prepare to become a professional property manager. It will give you the systems and tools needed to manage your tenants and properties with as few headaches as possible and for maximum profit.

OUTSOURCED MANAGEMENT

If you decide that self-management is not for you, this book will still be helpful if you choose to hire a professional property management company. The systems and tools outlined here will help you know what your management company should do to properly manage your investment properties. Your job is to essentially "manage" the manager. Without the knowledge this book presents, it will be hard to do that.

Whichever option you choose, start with the fundamental understanding that *managing residential rental properties is not easy and requires systems and tools and the skills to implement these systems.*

I hope this book is not the end of your learning journey but rather the beginning. Take the information and build on it with continuing education, learning what works for you and what does not. Build a better property management system for yourself and your investments.

Before we begin that journey, the next chapter will lay out the compelling thesis of why investing in rental properties will produce extraordinary financial results over the coming years.

As Andrew Carnegie said in the opening quote to this introduction, "More money has been made in real estate than all other investments combined." So let's get started!

CHAPTER 1

MY VIEW OF THE REAL ESTATE INVESTING AND RENTAL MARKET CONDITIONS OVER THE NEXT DECADE

"Real estate cannot be lost or stolen, nor can it be carried away. Purchased with common sense, paid for in full, and managed with reasonable care, it is about the safest investment in the world."

FRANKLIN DELANO ROOSEVELT, thirty-second President of the United States of America

We are all aware of the price distortions the pandemic has caused in the US over the past several years in both the real estate and rental markets. According to Zillow, as of March 2023, the average monthly rent throughout the country is $1,995, a startling 23.7% increase over the last two years. Real estate prices are also up a shocking 25.7% over the last two years, to an average home price of $334,994.

Most people will tell you these incredible price increases are a result of the pandemic. There is also a lot of chatter in the press and real estate blogs that real estate prices are in a "bubble" and are sure to go down over the coming years. The message being to avoid investing in real estate. Same with rental prices—"they" say rental prices must come down so the average person can afford their rent. But I would argue that opinion is way too simplistic and does not capture the "mega" trends occurring in the real estate and rental markets today.

MEGA TRENDS IN REAL ESTATE

Mega trends are powerful, transformative forces that could change the global economy, business, and society. They may occur over years or even decades and have been changing the way we live for centuries.[1] Think about electricity, the automobile, the Internet, and many other innovations that have caused large shifts in our society. Mega trends also happen in the real estate world, where massive changes are occurring in the way the US population wants to live. These changes will have a long-lasting impact on real estate and rental prices. Real estate investors and landlords need to be aware of these changes and use them appropriately in their decision-making.

US POPULATION AND GROWTH RATES

The US population is currently at about 330 million people and has been growing at around 1% per year over the last fifty years. The US population in 1960 was about 179 million and has almost doubled. That equates to nearly 100% growth in sixty years.

---

[1] BlackRock, "What Are Megatrends?," accessed May 24, 2023, https://www.blackrock.com/sg/en/investment-ideas/themes/megatrends.

At a 1% growth rate, the US population is growing at about 3.3 million people per year. There are projections that the growth rate will steadily drop to about 0.5% per year over the next fifty years. Regardless, the total population in the US will continue to increase over this period, and these people will need homes in which to live and raise families. This growing population is one of the keys to real estate investing as it puts constant upward pressure on real estate and rental prices.

HOME BUILDERS AND THE SHORTAGE OF US HOMES

According to research from Realtor.com, the US was short 5.24 million homes in 2022, and the problem is getting worse every year. The home shortage has increased by 1.4 million homes in just the last three years. In the previous ten years, 12.3 million American households have been formed, but only seven million new homes have been built.

We know that with an annual population growth of about 3.3 million people and the average US household size of about 2.3 people per home, home builders need to build about 1.5 million new homes annually just to keep up with population growth.

After the Great Recession, home builders built only 500,000 to 600,000 homes annually for several years, which caused the home shortage to accelerate. Over the last few years, home builders finally began to build enough homes to meet demand. Then the pandemic hit, which shut down home builders for twelve to eighteen months. Home builders are now faced with a supply chain crisis and rising interest rates, both of which have further negatively impacted their ability to meet housing demand.

There is also little evidence that home builders will be able to keep up with the demand for new homes over the next decade—let alone build enough homes to shrink the existing home shortage. The result will continue to be upward pressure on home prices and low rental vacancies. A perfect environment for real estate inventors.

RENTAL VACANCY RATES

Rental vacancy rates have decreased sharply over the last twelve years, from 11.1% in 2009 to 5.8% in 2022.[2] Vacancy rates have not been this low since the early 1980s. There are simply more people who want to rent than rental units available for rent, and this is pushing the vacancy rates to all-time lows.

RENTAL VACANCY RATE IN THE UNITED STATES

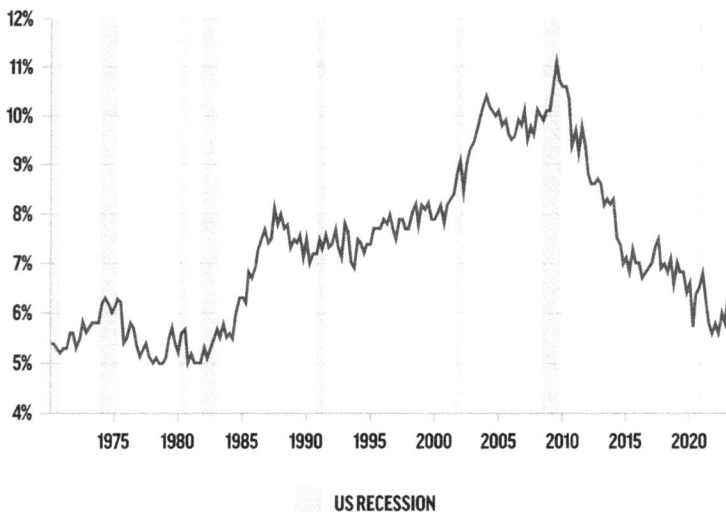

US RECESSION

Source: US Census Bureau
fred.stlouisfed.org

---

[2] FRED, Economic Research Federal Reserve Bank of St. Louis, accessed October 6, 2023, https://fred.stlouisfed.org/.

There are a number of factors causing this massive shortage in rental homes. As discussed previously, home builders are unable to build enough homes to meet demand. In addition, home builders tend to develop large single-family homes versus apartments. Single-family homes are easier to build and more profitable for home builders. This incentive to create more single-family homes is adding to the shortage of available rental units.

RENTING VERSUS OWNING A HOME

Another mega trend driving real estate and rental prices is the massive shift from homeowners to renters over the last ten years. In 2004, the homeownership rate peaked in the US at 69.4%. In 2022, that figure is down to 65.4%.[3] A 4% difference may not seem like much, but when accounting for 330 million Americans, it means that 13.2 million more people are now renters versus homeowners.

Add to this the fact that home prices are skyrocketing and interest rates have doubled in the last year, and this means fewer renters will be able to afford to buy a home and will stay as renters longer than in the past. As you can see from the associated chart provided by John Burns Real Estate Consulting, the cost of owning a home versus renting has never been higher.

Owning a home is currently estimated to cost about $830 per month more than renting, the opposite of ten years ago when owning a house was $200 per month less than renting. This will push people further to become renters, or remain renters, over the coming years. This mega trend has massive implications for

[3] FRED, Economic Research Federal Reserve Bank of St. Louis.

the country but will allow real estate investors tremendous upside opportunities in serving these renters.

HOME-OWNERSHIP RATE IN THE UNITED STATES

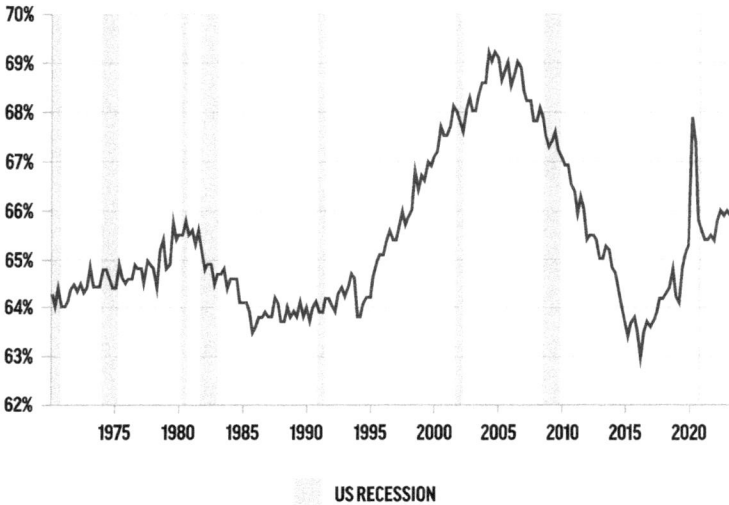

US RECESSION

Source: US Census Bureau
fred.stlouisfed.org

INFLATION AND NEW HOME COSTS

Inflation in the US has peaked at 9.1% as of June 2022. But the cost of construction materials is up 31.5% in the previous two years, which is the sharpest increase in the last fifty years.[4] These

---

[4] Christopher Rugaber, "US Consumer Price Growth Slowed Last Month as Inflation Shows Signs of Steady Decline," The Associated Press, June 12, 2023, https://apnews.com /article/inflation-prices-interest-rates-economy-federal-reserve-4c0ea8315ab90c1b832ef6 fa67dc0c7a; ABC, "ABC: Construction Materials Prices Rise 1% in January; Up 5% from a Year Ago," news release, February 16, 2023, https://www.abc.org/News-Media/News -Releases/abc-construction-materials-prices-rise-1-in-january-up-5-from-a-year-ago.

price increases in construction materials will drive new home prices much higher and are another factor pushing more people to remain as renters versus homebuyers. Despite what the *experts* might be saying, inflation is here to stay for many years.

LAND IS AT A PREMIUM

Another mega trend driving higher prices is the lack of available land on which to build. In some areas of the country—particularly in the Northeast—there is little land left to build homes or apartments. Even if a developer or home builder has land, getting permits, township approvals, environmental studies, and all the other paperwork takes years to complete. If a home builder purchased land today, it could be five to ten years before dirt is actually moved and they start to build new homes.

AVERAGE AGE OF US HOMES

According to the 2011 American Housing Survey, the median age of a home was forty-six years old. In the Northeast, many of these homes are over one hundred years old.[5] This means most US homes are outdated and are incredibly energy inefficient. They typically have one or one and a half bathrooms and maybe 1,200 square feet of living space. The modern home needs to be about 2,000 square feet and have two and a half to three bathrooms.

These homes cannot be fixed. They must eventually be torn down and rebuilt. Whereas one hundred years ago, builders may

---

[5] US Department of Housing and Urban Development, *American Housing Survey for the United States: 2011* (Washington, DC: US Department of Housing and Urban Development, US Department of Commerce, September 2013): 8, https://www.census .gov/content/dam/Census/library/publications/2013/demo/h150-11.pdf.

have built twenty houses in a city block, now they will rebuild to meet modern living styles and that same city block will only have ten to twelve homes.

CHANGING TRENDS TO LARGER HOMES

In 1980, the median size of a new home in the US was 1,595 square feet. Today that figure is nearly 2,386 square feet, accounting for an almost 50% increase.[6] According to US Census data, today's builders are building homes with four or more bedrooms, a gourmet kitchen, and a great room.[7] The implication is fewer homes are being built today, compared to the 1980s, on the same amount of land.

BUILD TO RENT TREND

Rental trends continue to change as more renters look for a lifestyle that offers larger homes, privacy, and less interaction with other people. As a result, single-family houses built to rent have become the hottest trend in housing over the last few years.

In 2013, only 1,740 single-family homes were built and designed to be rental properties. In 2022, that figure grew to 13,960.[8] According to a recent survey on RentCafe of 3,300 renters, as many as 78% said they were interested in living in a community

---

[6] Taylor Covington, "Supersized: Americans are Living in Bigger Houses with Fewer People," The Zebra, January 2, 2023, https://www.thezebra.com/resources/home/median -home-size-in-us/.

[7] Jesse Wade, "Share of Bedrooms in New Homes in 2021," National Association of Homebuilders, December 7, 2022, https://eyeonhousing.org/2022/12/share-of-bedrooms -in-new-homes-in-2021/.

[8] Alexandra Ciuntu, "Built-to-Rent Homes Expected to Hit All-Time High in 2022, Fueled by Need for Space and Privacy," RentCafe (blog), January 20, 2022, https://www .rentcafe.com/blog/rental-market/market-snapshots/built-to-rent-single-family-homes -double-in-2022/.

of single-family homes.[9] This trend will likely continue as renters' demands and preferences change, and builders will continue to change their designs to meet that demand.

Federal Reserve

My last section here is not really a mega trend but rather an observation. The Federal Reserve has increased interest rates over 5% in 2022 and early 2023 to counter the rampant high inflation. They are hoping to bring down inflation without causing a recession, commonly referred to as a "soft landing." But that is a tall order, and more than likely, these rate increases will push the US economy into a recession and may even, in the short run, cause home prices to flatten or trend slightly downward. But we also know that our politicians and the Federal Reserve do not like home prices going down.

If we entered into a recession and home prices were to go down—even by a small amount—there would be a push from our politicians to do *something* to stop this from going any further.

The Federal Reserve really only has one tool, which is to flood the economy with new money. If home prices were to come down, the Federal Reserve would quickly come to the rescue and add money into the economy, which would push real estate prices back up. It is what I call the "Real Estate Put," which means if real estate prices go down, Congress and the Federal Reserve will come to the rescue. This is merely my opinion, but history tells us that declining home prices will not be tolerated by the power players in Washington who will take swift corrective action.

---

[9] Ciuntu, "Built-to-Rent Homes Expected to Hit All-Time High in 2022."

A PERFECT STORM

These mega trends in the real estate market are a *perfect storm* of events that will drive real estate investment prices for years to come.

These mega trends include:

- Population growth of two to three million people per year
- Smaller households are causing fewer people to live in each home
- Home builders are unable to meet housing demand and slow down every time we have a recession
- Home affordability is causing more people to remain as renters
- Changing demand for larger homes and rental units puts pressure on home builders to build larger homes and reduces the number of homes on each parcel of land
- Record low vacancy rates causing upward pressure on rental prices
- Inflation running at 8% to 10% per year, with construction materials being priced much higher, thus pushing new home prices higher as well

I am not an economist but have been managing and investing in real estate for more than twenty years and have the experience to recognize these mega trends will drive real estate prices and rental rates higher for years to come. Could they go down for a short period of time? Yes, of course, but nobody can predict, with absolute certainty, what will happen at any given time. I believe a person holding real estate now, or planning to invest in real estate, will have extraordinary results over the next decade or two.

In the remaining chapters, you will discover the *nuts and bolts* of managing rental properties for maximum profits.

CHAPTER 2

PREPARING YOUR PROPERTY FOR MAXIMUM RENT

"You never get a second chance at a first impression."

—ANDREW GRANT, British Author

As a landlord it's critically important to understand how to prepare your rental units for rent. Your goal is to rent the property as quickly as possible for the maximum rent. The rental business is very simple in most cases—keep your vacancy periods to an absolute minimum and charge as much rent as the market will bear. So it is critical your unit is ready to rent and attractive to the best tenants.

Some landlords think that a quick coat of paint, cutting the grass, and a light cleaning is all that is needed to get a property rented. But today's renters have come to expect more and will demand a higher-quality property. This presents an opportunity for a landlord to make improvements, many of which do not cost much, to attract a higher-quality renter and a higher monthly rent.

This chapter describes many of the *little things* you can do as a landlord to enhance your property, so it appeals to today's renters. Several of them require little cost and can be done in an afternoon. Some are more expensive and may need to be done by a professional. But renting your property quickly and for a higher monthly rent will have a long-term return to you as a real estate investor.

CURB APPEAL—THE CRITICAL THIRTY SECONDS

Curb appeal is defined as the "general attractiveness of a house or apartment from the sidewalk to a prospective renter." That is why the most critical thirty seconds to a landlord is when a prospective renter gets out of their car and walks to the front door. If the "curb appeal" does not excite the prospective renter, or worse, turns them off, it is unlikely they will want to rent the property and you may have lost an excellent long-term tenant.

Things like overgrown weeds, a poorly cut lawn, an old car in the driveway, toys littering the sidewalks and pathway to the front door, poor lighting, chipped paint, and a loose doorknob will result in poor curb appeal. My experience is that if a person is turned off during these first thirty seconds, they have made their decision and the inside of the home or apartment may not matter at that point. A prospective tenant seldom changes their mind after a poor first impression. Game over!

It is critically important that you get people through these first thirty seconds with a positive mindset. Suppose the prospective tenants arrive at your property and see a carefully manicured lawn, attractive plants and bushes, a clean exterior, a well-lit pathway to the front door, and even a few decorative touches to the entryway. In this case, they will be excited to see more. It is also important to remember that good tenants have options because of their good credit scores or higher income, and you do not want to lose a good tenant because of poor curb appeal.

Let us go through several things you can do to add curb appeal.

POWER WASHING

Even after almost two decades in the real estate market, it still amazes me when I see properties listed for rent with several years' worth of grime or mold on their exteriors, driveways, and walkways. The exterior looks terrible and sends a message that the landlord does not care about the property. Would you want to rent from a landlord like that?

You can have your property power washed for about $400 to $800, and it will look 100% better. Power washing only takes a couple of hours and there are several options to get it done.

You can simply google "power washing" and your zip code. Numerous options of people and businesses will pop up with ratings and phone numbers. Call one or two and ask for an estimate to power wash your property.

Renting power washing equipment from a home equipment store can save money for landlords who prefer to do their own power washing. Or if you are a landlord with multiple properties, you could consider buying a power washer and doing it yourself or paying someone to do it. The investment into the equipment will pay for itself quickly.

Power washing will help your property show better and add years to the life of your exterior, walkways, and driveways. I recommend having your properties power washed yearly as part of a regular maintenance plan. If you do not, one season of sun, wind, debris, pollen, and snow (if you are in a cold-weather climate) can be enough to make a building look old and worn.

LANDSCAPING

Power washing your property is a great start, but you also need to look at your landscaping and determine if improvements might add curb appeal.

Too many landlords neglect to trim the bushes, pull the weeds, and replace dead plants in their landscaping. Again, these items do not cost much, but simply cleaning up your garden areas, trimming the bushes so they look neat, replacing dead plants, and adding mulch to your garden beds will dramatically impact the curb appeal of your property. These simple changes will tell the prospective tenant that the landlord takes great pride in their property and will continue to do so if they were to rent it. This is a powerful message and gets the prospective tenant excited about the property and looking forward to seeing the inside.

If you do not have the time to do the landscaping, pay professional landscapers to take care of the property. It will add long-term value to your property.

LIGHTING

One of the most inexpensive ways to improve curb appeal is simply to improve the lighting at the front of the home and any walkways. In the past, this might have required an electrician and would cost several thousand dollars. But today, you can purchase several small solar lights to light up a walkway. Most of them come in a four- or eight-pack for about $40 to $60 at your local home supply store. You can also order them from Amazon. There are many different color and style options to choose from. If you buy two of them you can put four solar lights on each side of the driveway or walkway, and it will look great if you are showing at night. There are even lights that are small and shaped like a hockey puck to embed into your grass, which allows lawn mowers to go directly over them.

You can also buy lights designed to point back at the house to light up the entire front of the property. This frames the house nicely to give it a warm and inviting glow. Proper lighting is a mood enhancer. Prospective tenants will feel welcomed where good lighting is present. Your existing tenants will also feel better about their living conditions and be more likely to stay long term.

THE ENTRYWAY

You may see a theme developing here, where these fixes tend to be simple items. They are not expensive, but they add a lot of value and may extend the life of many aspects of your property.

Most people would not consider the front door color to be significant, but it can greatly impact your curb appeal. According to a 2021 study by Zillow, homes with doors painted black sold for up to $6,000 more than other colors. The study also showed that pale pink had the opposite effect, and prospective buyers said they would pay an average of $6,516 less than expected.[10]

The Zillow study reflects the opinions of *homebuyers*, but we can assume that the opinions of *renters* are similar. If the front door of your property needs a fresh coat of paint, why not consider painting it black? Whatever color you choose, painting the front door will again show pride in your property and enhance the curb appeal.

---

[10] Zillow Group, "Is Your Front Door Black? Your Home Could Sell for $6,000 More," June 22, 2022, https://www.zillowgroup.com/news/best-front-door-color-2022/.

Additionally, not taking care of your door and paint as needed will result in permanent damage or dry rot. This means you may have to replace the front door sooner than expected. A small investment in paint is likely to pay off almost immediately.

If the front door paint is OK, a good cleaning with soap and water will make it pop and add curb appeal. For about $30, you also might want to add or replace the welcome mat so it looks fresh and clean.

In addition to the paint, ensure that the door's hardware is in good working order. If you turn the doorknob and it feels a little loose, get a screwdriver and tighten it until it feels secure. If something is broken or worn down on the hardware, replace it. Make sure all these items look attractive and are functioning as intended to continue the positive experience a prospective tenant gets while entering your property.

OTHER EASY-TO-UPGRADE ITEMS TO ADD CURB APPEAL

Power washing, landscaping, lighting, and maintaining the appearance of the entryway are fairly obvious ways to show prospective tenants that you take care of your property. There are several other *little things* that many people don't think of that can make a big difference in preparing your building for maximum rent. For example, the appearance of the mailbox will not make or break a deal, but it costs almost nothing in terms of money or time to paint it and make it consistent with the updated view of the rest of your property. Replace the mailbox—if needed—for added curb appeal with little cost.

If you are already doing some painting, take a look at the windows and trim of your property. Is it starting to crack or fade from sunlight? If so, give the window trim a quick touch-up to add shine to your freshly power-washed exterior.

After touching up the trim, think about adding planters to some of the windows. You can purchase flower boxes at any home improvement store. Not only do they add to the curb appeal, but tenants who enjoy gardening may appreciate the ability to have their favorite flowers or herbs right outside their windows.

If you are renting a single-family home, make sure the house numbers look updated. This is another low-cost, easy-to-implement item you can purchase at any home improvement store. By replacing old-style numbers with more modern-looking numbers you will add a finished and updated appearance to your property. House numbers cost only $8 to $10 each and will instantly improve the exterior. Also, consult your local township regulations, as many townships require house numbers on the back of the house as well as the front.

LITTLE THINGS ADD UP TO BIG ROI

All of these *little things* show prospective tenants that you care about the property and will maintain it when they move in. These small but high-impact items will enable you to charge an extra $50 to $200 per month for rent. A higher rent means your property will produce more monthly cash flow and will also increase the value of the property.

MULTIUNIT BUILDINGS

With multiunit buildings, you also need to consider the inside common areas, lobby, and hallways. Just like the outside, take a few minutes to stand in these locations to see if there is anything that might turn away a prospective tenant. For example, make sure the lobby and hallways have good lighting. Walking down a dark hallway is the quickest way to turn off a prospective tenant. People should feel safe and comfortable in a well-lit lobby and hallway. It might be as simple as replacing burnt-out light bulbs or it may require a professional electrician to add lights.

Smell is another big issue. People will react negatively if the inside of your property has any strong or foul odors. An overwhelming smell could be enough, on its own, to turn away a prospective tenant. First, determine if you have any strong odors and, second, determine how to eliminate the smell. You might try a simple handheld deodorizer and see if that does the job. If the spray does not kill the odor, try long-lasting deodorizers. Some deodorizers plug into a wall outlet and release a fragrance over a thirty- to-sixty-day period. But it is important that you neutralize any bad or foul odors before showing the vacant unit.

Clutter is another thing you cannot tolerate in a lobby or hallway. Tenants cannot use common-area hallways as storage space. You should have certain areas where tenants can store their belongings that are out of sight, such as a basement or outside area. Taking a prospective tenant down a hallway where they have to step around toys, shoes, and other debris is not going to be a presentation that leads to tenants wanting to live in your building. This could be especially troublesome for older people and those with disabilities.

Now that you have the outside and public areas looking good, let's turn our attention to the inside.

CARPETS, CABINETS, AND COUNTERS

Getting a unit ready to rent is not as simple as wiping down the countertops and sweeping the floors with a dust mop. Just like the outside, there are certain steps to ensure your unit makes the best possible presentation and tenants seeing the property will have a high desire to rent the unit.

First, the unit must be truly clean. Just like when you stay in a hotel, you do not want to get into your room and find out that it is *almost* clean. You want a clean room! Tenants are no different.

Many landlords have tried to clean their units themselves to save money. It almost always results in a unit that looks less than ready. Most landlords should hire professional cleaners to thoroughly clean the entire unit. Your job as the landlord is to inspect their work. Be sure the appliances are clean inside and outside and do not have any odors. The cabinets should also be clean inside and outside, with no crumbs or old food boxes. Bathrooms should be spotless. It should be obvious to anyone walking through the unit that it was professionally cleaned. People can tell just by noticing the fresh smell. You should also consider leaving a card on the counter from the cleaners that offers their phone number if anyone is unhappy with the cleaning and an offer to come back if they are not satisfied.

Kitchen appliances and counters are also important areas. Today's tenants prefer granite or similar materials, not Formica, for the kitchen counters. Higher-end countertops like granite are expensive, but if you want your rental units to achieve maximum rent, you might want to consider investing in this upgrade. Also, look at your appliances. If they are old or worn out, consider replacing them with a new appliance with a black or brushed-nickel exterior.

Carpets are a tricky area. Even newer carpets in relatively good condition must be professionally cleaned and shampooed. Carpets should smell good and have a pattern, so people can tell they have been professionally cleaned. However, most carpets over four or five years old should be replaced. I still see landlords trying to shampoo old, worn-out carpets, and they look no better after cleaning than they did before cleaning.

PAINT

Painting your property is another way to show off the unit if done correctly. If a tenant has been in an apartment for a few years or more, you will need to give *all* the rooms a fresh coat of paint. Some landlords want to just paint over a few cracks or spots on the wall and ignore the rest of the unit. When a wall has one or two patches of paint that look different from the rest of the wall, it can make the room look half-done and cheap, which can turn away tenants.

We recommend painting all the walls and ceilings of every unit every time a tenant who has lived in the unit for more than a year moves out. Ideally, you want everything to be a neutral color such as beige or light gray. We use a Sherwin-Williams paint called "Agreeable Gray" in most of our rental units. You can then also paint the trim in a high-gloss white to give the unit a modern and finished look. Resist the temptation to be bold or creative with your colors on interior walls.

CHANGE THE LOCKS

It is important to change the locks every time a tenant moves out of your property. In fact, some states and townships require the locks to be changed between each tenant. The standard doorknob and/or dead bolt locks still work fine, but there is a trend toward Bluetooth-enabled smart locks. Why not think about changing your locks to a "smart lock" to add technology-based enhanced value?

Smart locks, also called electronic or keyless entry systems, do not require a key to open. They use a four-digit code to open the lock. Some smart locks also allow the user to open the door with a phone app. The advantage of a smart lock is that you do not need to physically change the lock every time someone moves out. You can simply replace the code from the prior tenant. This can be a big cost savings. Also, you do not need to keep physical keys around and replace them all the time. Another advantage to smart locks is that they provide a modern look. When prospective tenants see a smart lock, they realize the owner is keeping up with advances in technology. It is a sign that the rest of the apartment will also be updated with modern conveniences.

There are a few disadvantages to smart locks. First, they tend to malfunction in cold climates. I operate near Philadelphia, and we have had some smart locks malfunction when we have extended periods of below-freezing conditions. Also, the batteries wear out and the locks will stop operating. Of course, this almost always happens late at night or on a weekend you are away. To prevent this, I would recommend giving the tenants extra batteries and showing them how to replace them. Also, most smart locks come with a physical key that can be used if the electronics of the lock are not working.

PEST CONTROL

Pests, or even signs of them, are a big issue when you are showing a property to prospective tenants. You do not want to lose a good tenant because your property has pest problems. This may seem obvious, but after managing thousands of rental units, it still surprises me how many landlords do not make absolutely sure there are no pests or signs of pests during property showings.

At a minimum, I would recommend arriving at your property fifteen minutes before any showing to open it up and quickly inspect it for signs of pests. If you find any, quickly clean up and make arrangements with your pest company to treat the property as soon as possible.

OTHER RENT-READY PREPARATIONS

Another important element of getting your property ready to rent is ensuring everything is in working order. Take some time to walk around and test all the lights, electrical outlets, faucets, toilets, showers, baths, and all appliances. Turn the heat and AC on to make sure they are working properly. Open and close all the windows to ensure they open and close easily. Test the garage door, if you have one, and all the other doors to make sure they operate as they should. Test the doorknobs and keys to be sure they function properly. Take the time to identify any problems before a tenant visits your property.

If your heating system is forced hot air, I recommend replacing the air filter. You should also buy four to six extra filters and leave them next to the heater, so your future tenants can change them. You can also send your tenants a reminder with a quick set of instructions or a video to show them how to do it every three to six months.

If your property has ceiling fans, be sure they are working properly and do not make noise when operating. Also, the dust that builds up on ceiling fans is one area we see missed a lot by cleaners. After your cleaners are done, be certain to check all your ceiling fans.

One final area is to be sure that the property has a working fire alarm and carbon monoxide alarms. Most townships require fire/carbon monoxide alarms in each bedroom and each level (including a basement). Check your township or city codes for information about where and how many of these alarms are required.

PROPERTY SHOWINGS TO PROSPECTIVE TENANTS

To turn prospective tenants into paying renters requires you to show them your apartment. Therefore, you must determine how you are going to show your property. There are various methods for doing this and each has advantages and disadvantages. Find out what will work best for you by asking some questions: Are you going to meet people at the property? Will you use lockboxes? What type of lockboxes will you use? Will you allow people to see the rental unit on their own? Do you need to meet everyone looking at the property?

KEYS

The simplest method to showing properties is to keep the keys to the unit and meet every prospective tenant at the property. The advantage of this system is you will get to meet every person who sees your property, which will enable you to ask questions that give you a sense for the type of person who might become your tenant. The disadvantage is you have to attend every showing and wait or hope they show up on time. Prospective tenants do not always tell the truth and the "no-show" percentage can be high at times.

LOCKBOXES

The standard lockbox is still the most common device used by realtors and landlords to store a key at the property. Most of these are set up like a basic combination lock with either push buttons or spin dials. The combination can consist of numbers or letters, and the lockbox will cost between $50 to $100 per device.

With a lockbox on the property, you arrange to meet a prospective tenant at the property, and the keys will be there waiting for you to open the door. You can also give the code to another realtor who may be showing the property to their clients without your needing to be there. I would recommend calling the realtor after the showing to ask how the showing went and to confirm they locked up when they left.

It is even possible for you to give the lockbox code to a prospective tenant and let them see the property themselves. This is called "self-showing." Although convenient, self-showings with a lockbox code have a number of issues. Fortunately, there is much better technology today to make self-showings much safer.

SMART LOCKBOXES

Smart lockboxes hold two to four keys and allow you to control access via Wi-Fi and a smartphone app. Typically, they cost $200 to $400 and offer several advantages over traditional lockboxes.

If you would like to do self-showings, smart lockboxes are designed with technology to perform self-showings as safely as possible. For example, a smart lockbox will give a prospective tenant a code to get the key, but the code will only work within thirty minutes before the scheduled showing to thirty minutes after the showing. Additionally, the prospective tenant will not get the code to open the box unless they are within one hundred feet of the front door. This prevents hackers from getting the code and allowing them to send unsuspecting tenants to your property.

A big advantage to a smart lockbox is that they allow people to view the property on their schedule without your involvement. As a landlord, you may also have a full-time job, and it may not be convenient for you to meet every prospective tenant at the property.

Renters—just like everyone else—can be fickle. Some of them show up forty-five minutes late; others call you twenty minutes after the scheduled time and tell you they will be there in another twenty minutes; and some people do not even bother to show up at all nor have the courtesy to call and tell you. Smart lockboxes can be convenient because you do not need to deal with the quirky tardiness of prospective tenants.

OPEN HOUSE

Open houses are another way to show your property. You can schedule open houses two or three times a week, including one on the weekend. If you want to be there, set a time like Saturday, 1:00 p.m. to 3:00 p.m., and allow prospective tenants to wander through the unit on their own. Offer to answer any questions at the end and provide a paper application or link to your online application.

AFTER YOUR PROPERTY IS PROPERLY PREPARED

In the next chapter, I will dive into pricing strategies for your rental properties. You will learn valuable tips about how much to charge and when you should increase the rent. Furthermore, you will also read about a few valuable resources to keep on hand that will help you to understand everything you need to know about rental prices.

CHAPTER 3

RENTAL PRICE STRATEGIES

R ent is the lifeblood of any landlord's rental business. In this chapter, I will detail how to determine what rent you should charge, how much rent to collect at move-in, how to increase the rent of existing tenants, and what additional charges you should be collecting from your tenants.

HOW TO DETERMINE YOUR RENTAL PRICE

If you are a new landlord, the first question that pops into your head is, "How much should I charge for rent?" This is an important question and has a huge impact on your financial success as a landlord. If you undercharge, you lose money each month, and you also will diminish the value of your property. Overcharge and the property will sit vacant for an extended period with no money coming in, and bad things tend to happen to vacant properties. So picking the right rental price is like the children's fable *The Three Little Bears,* where you want to pick the rent price that is "just right."

There are some simple techniques and online websites that will assist you in determining the rental price that is "just right" for your property. You may want to try several of them to get a range of rental prices that might work best for your property.

ASK THE NEIGHBORS

One of the simplest methods is to ask the neighbors around your rental property. Ask them what they think it might rent for or maybe what they are paying in rent. Nothing more complicated than that, and you may get some great information. Start a conversation and hand them your card, as they might also know somebody who could be interested in renting your property.

If the neighbor says they are paying $1,200 per month and your building is similar in beds, baths, square footage, appearance, and amenities, that amount might be a pretty good starting point. Even if your property has a slightly different number of beds or bathrooms, you can make small adjustments up or down to come up with a good starting point for your monthly rent. This is not an exact science, but it is quick, easy, and fairly accurate.

WHAT DID THE LAST TENANT PAY?

Another simple method is to look at what a previous tenant paid each month. Start there and adjust for local or national rent trends. Rents increased by 11.6% in 2021 and another 12% in 2022 on a national basis. Simply take the last rent paid and adjust up or down based on these trends.

THE 1% RULE

When trying to determine your rental price, you can use the "1% Rule," which states a rental property will rent for about 1% of its market value. This is a rule of thumb, as many areas will rent for more or less. My experience over the years, however, is that most properties will rent somewhere in the .8% to 1.2% range of the market value. If your property is worth $200,000, you could anticipate a monthly rent of approximately $2,000 with a range of $1,600 to $2,400 per month.

There are also many websites that are designed to help estimate the market rent. Some are better than others. But I recommend starting with the ones listed below.

ZILLOW

Zillow is by far the most popular website for looking at homes that are for sale. But they also list millions of properties for rent and offer a number of services to landlords.

Zillow uses an extensive computer algorithm called the Zestimate® for determining what a property might sell for. If you ask different people, they will have a variety of opinions on how accurate Zillow's tool is at predicting a home's sale price. But that is a deeper conversation for another day. Zillow also has an algorithm designed to predict rental prices known as the Rent Zestimate®. This is where you want to start your online process of determining the rental price for your property.

Start by going to Zillow.com, and on the first page there is a spot to enter your property address and then click the "search" button. Make sure that Zillow has the right property, and select your property. Then a report will pop up and you will proceed to the section titled "Your Home Value." You will see the Sale Zestimate for your property, but if you click on the "Zestimate History & Details" you will then be able to see your Rent Zestimate®. This is the amount Zillow thinks your property will rent for each month.

Zillow's Rent Zestimate® is a proprietary algorithm to determine the monthly rental price for a specific property. The Rent Zestimate® uses public property data and similar local properties listed for rent as part of the algorithm. There can be special features or differences between your property and Zillow's Rent Zestimate® that might lead Zillow's number to be inaccurate. However, if your property is a single-family home and similar to other properties in the area, it is generally accurate.

The Rent Zestimate® does have a couple of weaknesses. Zillow uses data from the prior six to twelve months. Since the pandemic, both real estate prices and rental prices are both surging up 15% to 20% across the US. But Zillow may be using data that is up to twelve months old. As a result, it may be using a lower price point to determine the Rent Zestimate®. In today's market, Zillow Rent Zestimate® may be on the low end compared to more recent activity. Also, it does not work nearly as well for multiunit dwellings. For example, you might type in an address and Zillow might return an estimate of $3,500 for a rent estimate. However, it does not factor in how many units are in the dwelling. If you own a three-unit building, it does not understand that there are three tenants versus a single-family home. So be aware of these weaknesses when doing your research.

DELVALPROPERTY.COM

Zillow is by far the largest real estate site, but there are many other online tools that can help you to discover the rental price for your property. For example, my company, Del Val Realty & Property Management, has a tool for landlords to determine the rental price at https://www.delvalproperty.com/philadelphia -property-management.

Similar to Zillow, you go to our website and enter the address, then provide some basic information like numbers of beds, bathrooms, square footage, and whether it is single or multifamily. From that input, you get a much more detailed six- or seven-page *Rental Property Analysis Report*, showing the estimated rental price but many other important facts as well. These additional items include a list of the actual "similar" properties it used as comps and charts showing the five-year trend in pricing and time to rent properties.

REDFIN

Another site similar to Zillow is Redfin.com. You simply go to their website and drop in the property address, and a rental price estimate will pop up on-screen. Where Zillow gives a single number, Redfin will give a range of where they think the rent price will land.

My recommendation is to experiment using these various price strategies to acquire a range for your property. Whatever tool you use and whatever amount you settle on, this is the starting point and ultimately the real market will dictate where your rent will fall.

WHAT IS THE RIGHT RENTAL PRICE?

Once you start to advertise your property on Zillow and other online sites, you should expect somewhere between six to ten inquiries per week. Inquiries can be calls, texts, or emails about your property. If you have priced it right, the six-to-ten-inquiries range will confirm you are priced correctly. But if your ads are producing less than this amount, it may sit vacant longer than needed. If you are getting more than this amount, it may mean your price is too low and you may need to adjust upward to capture as much rent as possible. Again, this is not an exact science, but these guidelines should steer you close to the right number.

Ultimately, the choice is yours on what you charge for rent. You can use any of the previously mentioned tools to help you come to that decision. Once you establish a starting point for your rent, the next question becomes when rent will be due and how much you should demand upfront before the tenant moves in.

Case Study

I selected a property we manage to illustrate how these different pricing strategies would work in the real world. The property is a single-family home with four bedrooms in an area with mostly single-family homes. Here are the results:

Prior Tenant—The prior tenant was paying $2,395 per month for rent, which was last increased in 2021. Adjusting for national rent trends at about 12%, this would indicate a rental price of $2,682.

1% Rule—This property is valued at around $338,300. Abiding by the 1% Rule would indicate that the rental price should be $3,383.

Zillow—Zillow has the Rent Zestimate at $2,447.

Del Val Website—Our website determined a rental price of $2,571.

Redfin—Redfin gave us a price range of $2,379 to $2,599.

The 1% Rule seems to be an outlier, but if we take the other four methods, they average to $2,535 per month.

Conclusion—We just rented this property within the last thirty days for $2,595. This shows that the pricing strategies above did an outstanding job at predicting the market rent.

WHAT MONIES SHOULD BE COLLECTED UPFRONT?

Prior to advertising your vacant property, you must determine what money you are going to collect up front before a tenant moves in. Our standard lease requires the full first month's rent and two months of rent as a security deposit. There could be other fees such as a pet fee or pet security, but we will deal with that later in this book. You also need to review what your state rules are regarding how much security you are allowed to collect.

One thing we get asked a lot is if a tenant moves in the middle of the month, do we allow the tenant to prorate the rent for the first month? For example, if the rent is $1,000 and they want to move in on the sixteenth of a month, can they pay $500 to move in? We do not permit prorated rent for the first month, and I would recommend you not allow this practice.

We require the full first month of rent and we prorate the second month. You do not want someone moving in on the thirtieth of the month and paying just one day of rent. This is also a small test to separate weaker tenants from the better ones. If the tenants can pay the full three months of rent at move-in, it shows that they have better money management skills than a tenant who can pay the two months' security and just a small prorated rent.

Our standard lease requires tenants to pay the rent on the first of every month. As a landlord, you want to have systems that make things as simple as possible. Other landlords may be more flexible and allow the tenant to pay on odd days of the month, but we do not believe this is a best practice.

WHEN TO RAISE THE RENT AND BY HOW MUCH

If you are filling a vacant unit, we have outlined numerous pricing strategies above to maximize the rent. But if you have a current tenant in your property, how, when, and by how much should you increase the rent when the lease term ends? The first rule to remember when it comes to raising rent is that if you use a one-year lease term, you should increase the rent every time the lease term ends. How much should you raise the rent? You need to analyze local and national trends and raise the rent accordingly.

According to Zumper's Annual Rent Report, 2021 showed an average rental price increase of 11.6% for one-bedroom units and 13.6% for two-bedroom units.[11] But these are national numbers.

---

[11] Zumper, *Annual Rent Report: 2021* (Zumper, 2021): 2, https://www.zumper.com/blog/zumper-2021-annual-rent-report/#.

If you want to get the amounts for your town, visit www.zumper.com. On their site, they show the rent increases for about fifty cities throughout the US. You can find your city on their list and get a more focused rent increase percentage in your town versus relying on a national number.

It is a natural tendency for a landlord to want to "be nice" and cut a break for good tenants who have been with them for a long time by not increasing the rent or increasing it less than local trends. However, the best way to maximize profits is to raise rent every year in line with local and national rent trends.

Most real estate experts agree that investment property values are directly related to their rental income. The rule of thumb is that most properties are worth approximately one hundred times the monthly rent (the 1% Rule in reverse). Therefore, if your property is currently rented for $1,000 and you increase the rent by 3%, which is only $30 per month, the value of your property will increase by $3,000. Consequently, the opposite is also true. If you do not raise the rent for a few years, your rent will fall behind, and it will negatively impact your property value. We see this often with private landlords who do not keep their rents up with market trends. When they attempt to sell the property, they find that buyers are not willing to pay full asking price.

The negative effect of not raising rents is compounded when you realize that you have lost money in two ways. First: the money left on the table when you sell your property. Second: the cumulative rent you have lost every month in which you did not maximize the potential for profit. Part of being a professional landlord is doing the things that might not be popular but are required to maximize your investment value.

HOW TO COMMUNICATE RENT INCREASES TO TENANTS

If you do plan to increase the rent it is critical that you properly notify the tenant. You should send them a Rent Increase Notice to inform them of the new rent amount and the date on which it will increase. Some states also require landlords to provide a notice within a certain time frame to avoid breaking local landlord–tenant laws. But as a general rule I would plan to let the tenants know sixty to ninety days prior to the increase date. We have provided a sample copy of a Lease Renewal Addendum in Appendix B, which we use when renewing a lease and increasing the rent.

IT IS TIME TO LET PEOPLE KNOW YOU HAVE A UNIT FOR RENT

Now that you know the importance of developing a good rental price strategy, it is time to dive into how to advertise your property. After all, you will not collect any rent if prospective renters do not know you have a potential property for rent.

CHAPTER 4

HOW TO ADVERTISE YOUR RENTAL PROPERTY ONLINE AND OFFLINE

Advertising rental properties has dramatically changed over the last few decades. The days of going into a real estate office to look at outdated books of property listings are long gone (in fact, most people under forty will not even know what I am talking about). The classified section of a local newspaper and the Sunday drive around town trying to spot a "For Rent" sign in a nice neighborhood have also gone the way of the outdated property listing books.

Like so many things in our lives, the Internet has significantly changed the way people search for rental properties. In particular, most rental property searches are happening on smartphones.

Pew Research reports that 85% of Americans owned smartphones in 2021.[12] With immediate access to things like online

---

[12] Chris Kolmar, "25+ Incredible US Smartphone Industry Statistics [2023]: How Many Americans Have Smartphones," Zippia, March 2, 2023, https://www.zippia.com/advice/us-smartphone-industry-statistics/#.

reviews, photos, 360 virtual tours and room dimensions, it is no wonder tenants are abandoning traditional rental marketing tactics like real estate signage and newspaper ads. According to a Zillow Group Report, 73% of renters use online resources to find a home— and only 11% report using print ads.[13]

This shift in the way renters look for available properties is another example of how landlords need to evolve with the times or risk getting left behind.

When landlords advertised in the local newspaper, they could use a little poetic license. For example, the phrases "tree-lined street" and "a great place to raise a family" were used frequently. But that is *not* how people look for properties online. Today, people type keywords into a rental listing site like Zillow such as "home for rent near xxx college." They will not use the words "tree-lined street" in these searches.

Here is a list of common search words you can include in your titles and body of your rental ads:

- Town, city, or zip code
- Local universities or colleges
- Large employers in the area
- Well-known landmarks
- Bus/trolley/train stops
- Section 8 OK
- Pet friendly
- Finished basement

---

[13] Alycia Lucio, "How to Find Renters," Zillow Resources, Zillow, February 21, 2020, https://www.zillow.com/rental-manager/resources/how-to-find-renters/.

- In-ground, heated pool
- Central air conditioning

That is just a sampling of typical keyword searches from people who are looking to rent a property. They might want to live in a certain area or near a certain college or workplace, or maybe they are tired of sweating through hot summers and would do anything for a reasonably priced apartment with central air conditioning. You must keep the wants and needs of today's tenants in mind when listing your property for rent, as your ads need to have keywords that showcase these features.

With that knowledge in hand, you now need to know where and how to advertise your residential properties for rent.

ONLINE ADVERTISING SOURCES

There are several options to advertise your rental property online. Of course, Zillow is the big dog in this area as well. But there are a few other options you may want to use when advertising your rental properties.

ZILLOW RENTAL MANAGER

If you are looking for pure volume for your rental property advertisement, Zillow Rental Manager is the best starting point. Zillow Rental Manager and its partner sites, Trulia and HotPads, receive a combined average of 68 million users per month. Zillow's market research indicates that over 76% of people start their apartment search online.[14] One of the biggest advantages to using Zillow Rental Manager is that when you place an ad with them, they will also syndicate (feed) your ad to both Trulia and Hot Pads.

Your first listing with Zillow Rental Manager is free. All additional ads will cost $9.99 per week per unit. In my opinion, this fee is well worth the price for the exposure your properties will receive. In today's hot rental market you may only need four to six weeks to find an acceptable tenant.

Zillow Rental Manager also offers a number of other services you may want to consider (I would check the pricing as it may change from time to time). The site offers online rental application and tenant screening for $29 paid by the tenant (so free to landlords). Other services include online lease signing (similar to DocuSign), online rent collection, and a 3D tour software tool. These extras are designed to give you—the landlord—more of a one-stop shopping destination.

ZUMPER

Zumper caters to both landlords and tenants. Renters can search by their top criteria, while landlords can stipulate credit score minimums for applicants using two-way matching. Adding listings to Zumper is free, and listings will also be syndicated to PadMapper and Facebook Marketplace.

Zumper may not yet have the reach of Zillow, but it is gaining momentum. It originated in 2011, and most of us still had not heard of it as recently as 2017. As a professional property manager

---

[14] Manny Garcia, "Renters: Results from the Zillow Consumer Housing Trends Report 2022," Zillow Research, Zillow, July 27, 2022, https://www.zillow.com/research/renters -consumer-housing-trends-report-2022-31265/.

we advertise forty to sixty properties per month, and Zumper has grown enormously as a lead source for our rental properties. It is becoming a real powerhouse in the rental market. After all, nobody had heard of Zillow, Facebook, or YouTube at one time either.

CRAIGSLIST

Craigslist is still one of the most popular sites on the Internet for classified ads including rental ads. Craigslist includes a section for posting ads for apartments and housing for rent in just about every city in America. Craigslist is widely used by both landlords and tenants alike, but has a big red flag as it is full of scammers, and people will take your ad, copy it, and reduce the price so they can get people to send them application fees and first month's rent. Craigslist can be effective but you should be fully aware of the risks involved.

Del Val is not currently using Craiglist due to these problems and for the safety of our tenants.

APARTMENTS.COM

The Apartments.com network consists of seven different partner sites whose combined reach is estimated at 70 million per month. Check their website, as they offer several different options for pricing, allowing you to buy several ads in a bulk package. The price can be quite high, however, if you want your ads to appear near the first page. Apartments.com also offers many of the same extra services that Zillow offers.

REALTOR.COM NETWORK

The Realtor.com network claims their monthly traffic is currently around 86 million users and growing quickly. But Realtor.com is mostly known as a site to buy properties. So most of that traffic is likely prospective buyers, not renters.

WALK SCORE

When using the site Walk Score, your property will be ranked based on its proximity to grocery stores, business districts, and other attractions that encourage non-car commuting.

When tenants are searching for shorter commutes, dining, and entertainment possibilities within a short distance, a strong walk score can be a shorthand for a high desirability apartment. In addition, you can attach badges with your property's walk score to your listings to promote its great location.

If you are renting a property in a major metropolitan area, it makes a lot of sense to use Walk Score. Big cities like Philadelphia, Boston, Chicago, New York City, Los Angeles, and others have downtown areas that get a lot of traffic. Renters in those areas want access to the clubs, restaurants, coffee shops, retail centers, other commerce locations, and public transportation to be within walking distance of their apartment.

SOCIAL MEDIA

According to the Pew Research Center, 72% of American adults use some form of social media. The most popular platforms are YouTube, with 73% of adults using it, followed by Facebook (69%), and Instagram (37%).[15] With numbers like that, social media would seem to be a natural fit for real estate advertising, yet it remains a mostly untapped resource for landlords.

---

[15] Brooke Auxier and Monica Anderson, "Social Media Use in 2021," Pew Research Center, April 7, 2021, https://www.pewresearch.org/internet/2021/04/07/social-media-use-in-2021/.

The social media platform that comes the closest to being an effective place to list your rental property is Facebook Marketplace. This is still not a traditional listing website, but it can increase the visibility of a rental property's advertisement. Facebook Marketplace is best known for generating quick responses to rental ads.

However, our experience with Facebook Marketplace is that it is loaded with scammers trying to steal ads, post a property they do not own for rent, replace the contact information with their own untraceable info, and attempt to collect application fees or rent from an unsuspecting victim.

To be safe, I do not recommend using Facebook Marketplace until something changes around their security measures.

ONLINE ADVERTISING TIPS

Now that you know all about *where* to advertise your residential rental property, you need to know *how* to advertise it. The next few subsections go over best practices for advertisement techniques in the property rental business.

HOW TO WRITE EFFECTIVE HEADLINES

The headline is important because it is how your rental property advertisement gets noticed. Effective headlines have three components:

1. **A key feature**—This could be a good school district, finished basement, large yard, etc.
2. **The number of bedrooms**—If you are listing a house, write "4-bedroom house." If you are listing an apartment, write "2-bedroom apartment."

3. **The area**—You can include the town, zip code, or other sub-geographic zone.

By writing an effective headline, you are trying to meet the keyword searches of your prospective renters. As I mentioned earlier, people do not look for "tree-lined streets" or "great place to raise a family" anymore.

People search by the three criteria listed here for an effective headline. They get in front of their computer or smartphone and type in "2-bedroom apartment in downtown Philadelphia." If you write an effective headline, your listing will appear for that person. The following are some samples of effective headlines we use:

- Nicely Updated 2 Bedroom Condo For Rent—xxx E. Lancaster Avenue—Available now in the Main Line area!
- Well-maintained 3-Story, Brick, End-of-Row Home for Rent—xxx Astor Street—West End Norristown.
- Nicely Renovated 3-Bedroom Row Home For Rent— xxx Pennell Street—Available in Chester Now!
- Nicely Updated 3-Bedroom Twin Home For Rent— xxx Fitzwilliams Road, Bryn Mawr (Radnor Township).
- Newly Renovated Contemporary 2-Bedroom Apartment For Rent Now—xxxx S. Broad Street, 2nd FL—City Living at its Best!—Newbold /Passyunk Square area.

In the age of texting and direct messaging, people do not read full sentences anymore, so there is no longer a need for poetic license in an effective property rental listing. Tell people about the key features, list the number of bedrooms, and give them the location. This will catch their attention and generate clicks for more information, such as details and photos.

HOW TO WRITE EFFECTIVE BODY TEXT

Once you have caught the attention of the right people, you can provide some detail in the body text. Even here, however, you want to stick to the facts. Tell them the square footage, the parking situation, exterior features like patios and porches, and of course, the price.

Effective body text should also include the nearby major roads, highways, shopping centers, universities, and employers. You might also want to include the payment terms and lease requirements. Finally, you may want to include showing instructions as well.

The body text should use bullet points to provide short and concise information rather than full sentences. In this way, people can scan the information rather than reading it word for word.

There is no need to sugarcoat anything in a property rental advertisement, so if there is something that might turn off certain renters, you should think about including it in the listing. This may sound counterintuitive, but there is no sense in scheduling a showing for a third-floor apartment in a building with no elevator for someone who is disabled or just does not want that inconvenience of walking steps. If that is the case, you should include "third floor, no elevator" in the listing. That way, you do not waste anyone's time, including your own.

After you have mastered the written word to craft a catchy headline and effective supporting body text, it is time to include the right pictures. They say a picture is worth a thousand words, but how much rent is it worth?

HOW TO TAKE PHOTOS/VIDEOS

Including ten to twenty photos in online listings is crucial to the effectiveness of your rental property advertising. Airbnb recently reported that they saw a 20% increase in properties being booked with high-quality photos.[16]

Several years ago, you would need a good camera that might cost $500 to $1,000 with a wide-angle lens to take high-quality photos. Today, the camera on your smartphone is good enough with the below strategies to take high-quality photos.

The most important thing to remember when taking photos is to make sure you get every room. If prospective renters do not see any photos of a bedroom or bathroom, they will suspect there is something seriously undesirable about the apartment. So put those people at ease by taking plenty of photos and trying to get at least one of every room.

It is equally important to take photos of the property's exterior. People want to know what the property looks like from both the inside and the outside. Take a picture of the front door. If you are doing a video, walk into the front door, turn around and scan the section of the street around your property. Even if the street view is not as pleasant as you want it to be, it is good for the tenant to know this. Once again, you do not want to waste everyone's time by scheduling a showing only to have the person look around the surrounding area and say to themselves, "There is no way I am living on this street."

---

[16] Airbnb Administrator, "Help Boost Listing Performance with Quality Photos," Community Center, Airbnb, June 8, 2018, https://community.withairbnb.com/t5/Airbnb -updates/Help-boost-listing-performance-with-quality-photos/td-p/776384.

I would also recommend taking photos on a sunny day to capture as much light as possible. Maximizing the light evokes a more pleasant feeling, so open up the curtains and let the light shine through. Remove any clutter before taking photos. And remember the old real estate agent adage, be sure the toilet seats are down.

Do not take any photos of mirrors, because they can lead to a confusing view or even make the space look smaller than it actually is. Leave people out of the pictures as well. There is no need to capture a family sitting at the dinner table in a property listing.

To avoid any odd or unbalanced photos, make sure you keep the camera steady. If this is a problem for any reason, you should buy a tripod. You also want to make sure your photos are at least 300 by 500 pixels. If possible, 600 by 800 is best, but most listing sites will require a minimum of 300 by 500. You can also use online photo-editing sites to add brightness or crop photos to look better.

You do not need to be a professional photographer to take effective pictures or video for your rental property listing. Today's technology enables anybody to take high-quality photos or video without using expensive equipment or enlisting the services of a photographer. However, it is always a good idea to take advantage of the best aspects of your property. If there is a nice-looking tree on the side of the property, try to include a picture of it framing the house. If there are some attractive flowers or plantings in the front yard, take a picture with the flowers highlighting the front of the house. If the property has a big lawn in the backyard, get a picture of that. You want to include all the best features of the property.

HOW TO USE VIRTUAL TOURS

Adding a virtual tour to your rental ads can make a big difference in the number of prospective tenants that see your listing and also how quickly you can rent a vacant property. Virtual tours differ in quality and price from one application to the next. Zillow's 360 Home Tour is basic, but it is free.

You download the Zillow 360 app on your smartphone and walk into each room of your rental property, and the website prompts you to begin taking photos. You snap a picture every few seconds from a different angle or perspective of each room. When you are done, the application takes the accumulation of these photos and creates a virtual tour.

There are much better quality products available such as Matterport, which involves buying a high-end camera for several thousand dollars and uploading videos to their service.

Matterport is a pricey investment, but it does a great job of going room to room and creating a beautiful, smooth video that includes the dimensions and schematics for each room. That way, a viewer can watch the video and say, "Oh, my couch will fit perfectly right along that wall, and I can put the television on the other side of the room."

At one end of the virtual tour spectrum of service providers, you have Zillow, which is free but clunky in its presentation. At the other end is Matterport, which is expensive (around $3,000 for the camera today) but provides that elite quality that you might be looking for if you have a very high-end rental property. Various options exist in between as well. For example, I have used a service that also involved buying a camera, but the cost was only about $500.

VIRTUAL STAGING

One innovative tool that has gained popularity in recent years is virtual staging. Virtual staging is the process of creating a 3D model of the space and adding furniture, decor, and other features to make it look more appealing. This technology allows landlords to showcase their properties as they might look furnished without the cost and headache of dealing with staging companies.

There are several websites that offer virtual staging services for landlords. One popular option is PadStyler, which offers virtual staging for both residential and commercial properties. Another website is BoxBrownie, which offers virtual staging and other real estate photo-editing services. Finally, there is roOomy, which specializes in virtual staging and 3D modeling for real estate.

I suspect virtual staging will become more and more popular as it improves the quality and the costs come down.

Using AI-Generated Photo-Editing Sites

As a landlord, presenting your rental property in the best possible light is essential to attracting prospective tenants. One effective way to achieve this is through the use of artificial intelligence (AI) photo-editing sites.

These sites use advanced algorithms and machine learning techniques to enhance and improve your rental property photos, resulting in visually appealing and attractive images. They can adjust the brightness, contrast, color balance, and other aspects of your photos to make them more appealing to potential renters.

Using AI photo-editing sites can save landlords a significant amount of time and effort. Instead of spending hours manually editing each photo, they can simply upload them to the platform and let the AI do the work.

In addition to improving the visual appeal of your rental property photos, AI photo-editing sites can also help to highlight the property's key features. For example, they can bring out the details of a beautiful kitchen or highlight the spaciousness of a living room. This can make your rental property stand out from others and attract more potential tenants.

TIMING

When should you post your ads? We post our ads as soon as our Marketing Department has them ready. Other landlords like to time the appearance of their listings in an effort that they believe will optimize effectiveness. According to Zillow's Rentals Resources Center, Thursdays are the ideal day to post because renters want to schedule tours for the upcoming weekend.

ON-SITE "FOR RENT" SIGNS

Although almost all rental properties are listed online these days, there is some level of on-site marketing. Whereas the old-fashioned "For Rent" sign is not as effective as it used to be, it still plays a role in getting your property rented to the right person.

Because only people nearby see the "For Rent" sign, it will reach a smaller group of potential tenants. As a result, these signs work best on a high-volume street. However, there are a few things you can do to improve their effectiveness.

Like anything else that originated several decades ago, property rental signage has changed. You still want to include basic information like a phone number and exactly what it is that is being rented, e.g., "1-Bed Apt. for Rent." Today, you might want to include a number to text and a QR code as well. The phone number you leave could lead to an automated message that provides a two or three-minute description of the apartment and next steps needed if they would like to schedule a visit. The same principle applies with the text or QR code; those would lead to a website offering pictures and other details to schedule a tour of the home or apartment.

Also, consider the colors of your sign. I would recommend dark backgrounds such as navy blue, dark gray, or even black with white or yellow letters. These combinations offer high-contrast signage that can be seen much farther away than white backgrounds.

If the street is a high-speed street, you may need to put up two signs that are at forty-five-degree angles to the street. Cars traveling at high speeds are much more likely to see a sign at this angle versus one that is parallel to the street. This way, you also cover traffic coming from both directions.

There is an argument for not putting up a "For Rent" sign in front of your property as it tells the world that the unit is vacant. In some impoverished areas, this is a sign to tell local drug users that if they can find a way to get into the apartment, they have a safe place to gather.

At times, I have been instructed by local law enforcement not to put a "For Rent" sign in front of a property because it is an open invitation for crime. Therefore, we use these signs on a limited basis.

MARKETING AN OCCUPIED APARTMENT

When you know a tenant is moving out, many landlords want to get the apartment rented again as soon as possible. In a particularly hot market, you will likely get many requests to rent your apartment before it is vacated. Even in non-pandemic times, this is a difficult task. The existing tenant may have a crying baby, a barking dog, dishes piled up in the sink, and toys littered across the floor in every room. This is not an ideal situation, but if there is enough demand in the area, some people may overlook these things and want to rent the place anyway.

If you have prospective tenants lined up and waiting to see the apartment and you are trying to get it rented immediately after a move-out, you must work with the existing tenant. Arrange a block of two or three hours when they will be out of the apartment while you show the apartment.

In my experience, it is almost always better to tell prospective applicants that they can only see the apartment once it is vacant. If your previous tenant is scheduled to move out on July 31, tell people that they can see the place on or after August 5 so you have time to get the apartment cleaned and get it ready for showings.

ADVERTISING FOR SECTION 8 TENANTS

The housing choice voucher program is a federal government program for assisting low-income families, the elderly, and the disabled to find housing. It is commonly referred to as Section 8. Many landlords perceive the idea of renting to Section 8 tenants as undesirable due to many factors. But there are several big advantages to working with your local Section 8 housing office.

Section 8 tenants offer consistent guaranteed rent payments from the government, so it takes a lot of the payment risk out of the equation. Also, there is high demand for Section 8 housing in most cities. There will be more individuals with Section 8 vouchers than there are available units.

In addition to guaranteed rent, Section 8 does a lot of the work for the landlord, as they have a rigorous application process. Renters who qualify usually need to show that they will be decent tenants, so this is another big advantage to your properties being Section 8 friendly.

A disadvantage to Section 8 rentals is that the government controls the rent increases. When renting to Section 8 tenants, you will most likely have a one- or two-year lease agreement. At the end of the lease term, you can ask to raise the rent, but the government may only allow a small increase, typically 2% or 3%.

Another disadvantage is that the government will stop any payments if the tenant complains of a broken life-safety item in the apartment, like a heater or a refrigerator. Even if you get it fixed as soon as possible, the government will abate the rent for as long as the broken system is not functioning. For example, if the tenant did not have a working refrigerator for seven days, you will collect zero rent for those seven days.

When advertising for Section 8 tenants there are a couple of tips that will help your ads get a better response. To start, make sure your online ads have phrases like "Section 8 Welcome" or "Section 8 OK." But do not use something like "Section 8 Only." As a landlord, it is better to err on the side of inclusivity, not exclusivity. By excluding anyone you could be in violation of the Fair Housing rules.

Almost all big cities will have a local Section 8 office that administers the program for that area. If you would like to rent to Section 8 tenants, call your local office and ask them for any ideas on how to reach their clients. Also, ask if they have a list of available properties on which you can get your property listed. Generally, these offices can be hard to get a real person on the phone, but if you do, they will be very helpful with information and tips on how to help their clients.

When considering Section 8 tenants, you need to weigh the advantages against the disadvantages. Some landlords love the idea of guaranteed rent being paid on time. It virtually eliminates economic risk. Other landlords, however, prefer to assume a little risk for control over their rental increases, which as I stated earlier, is a key to maximizing profits.

Now that you know about Section 8 and the ins and outs of creating an effective advertisement for your rental property, it is time to learn the tips and strategies I have acquired in my many years of experience to properly screen tenants and select the best choice for your property.

CHAPTER 5

THE TENANT APPLICATION AND SCREENING PROCESS

T he next step to maximize profits from your residential rental properties is to develop a system for handling applications and tenant screenings. Finding good tenants is critical to the success of any real estate investing business. If you have good tenants, real estate investing is a great business. But having bad tenants can make things very difficult. And the best way to find good tenants is through your application and tenant-selection process.

The rental application and tenant-screening process collects financial information, criminal and background checks, and the renter's background and prior rental history. By reviewing this information, you can make a much better decision to accept or decline an application. No system is perfect, but a well-thought-out application process will tremendously improve the odds of selecting good tenants.

It is also important that your tenant application and screening process complies with the federal Fair Housing Act that prevents discrimination against tenants. This is an area where a lot of landlords make mistakes and get themselves into trouble with the federal government.

Sample Application in the Back

You will find a sample paper application in Appendix C at the end of the book. While most landlords now use online applications, the sample still provides a visual aid to help you understand how the pieces fit together.

THE APPLICATION PROCESS

In the past, most people filled out paper applications and submitted them with supporting documents like pay stubs, bank statements, and tax returns. The landlord would then review all the information and make a decision to accept or decline the applicant. Today, most companies use online applications that have many advantages over the paper version.

The benefits of online applications include less clutter in your office, better organization, the ability to "score" applications, and a more convenient process for applicants. Today there are dozens of online application services you can select including Zillow Rental Manager, which charges $29 per application.

The average application fee is between $35 and $70, and at Del Val we charge $50 per person. The application fees help offset the cost to run a credit report, which is typically about $20 to $30 per person, and your time to collect and review the application. We do not consider application fees as a profit center, but more as a vital tool to help select the best tenants.

Everyone over the age of eighteen who wishes to live in the apartment must fill out an application. If a married couple is moving in together, they must each submit their own application. The same rule should apply to all roommates (and cosigners if applicable). You want all people living in the unit to complete an application so you have a complete picture of the person(s) leasing your property.

After collecting the application and all the necessary documentation, the next step is to go through a systematic approval process.

THE APPROVAL PROCESS

It is crucial to approve tenant applications in order to find the best tenants, while also being in compliance with Fair Housing regulations. A landlord should have a scoring system and rules for accepting or declining applicants. This way the landlords can be sure they are treating all applicants the same as required under the Fair Housing rules.

An approval process and scoring system can include income-to-rent ratio, past evictions, criminal records, credit scores, and more. As part of your approval process you may also want to consider the number of people legally permitted to live in the unit, a smoking policy, and how to handle cosigners or financial guarantors.

> Del Val does not always accept the *first* applicant that meets our criteria; we give the apartment to the *best* applicant if we have received multiple applications.

Del Val has two primary factors that we use to approve or decline an applicant. They include the *Income-to-Rent Ratio* and the *NTN Score*.

INCOME-TO-RENT RATIO

One of the two primary factors we use to evaluate an applicant is the Income-to-Rent Ratio. To calculate the Income-to-Rent Ratio, simply divide the applicant's combined monthly gross income (before taxes) by the rent you are charging. For example, if the applicant's combined gross monthly income is $3,750 and your rent is $1,000, that applicant's Income-to-Rent Ratio would be 3.75.

We require an applicant to have an Income-to-Rent Ratio of 3.0 or higher. Now you may be tempted to approve a 2.8 or 2.9, but be careful in accepting anything that is slightly below your required minimum as it would violate your application process.

If another applicant's gross monthly income is $2,500 and your rent is $1,000, their Income-to-Rent Ratio is 2.5 and would not meet our required 3.0 threshold, and the applicant would be declined.

THE NATIONAL TENANT NETWORK SCORING SYSTEM

The second primary criteria we use in the application-approval process is the NTN Score. Del Val uses an outside company called National Tenant Network (NTN) to process our applications. NTN produces a Decision Point Plus Report, which is a three-to-five-page report that includes an NTN Score, which is a number between 1 and 100 that is much more comprehensive than just a credit rating. The NTN Score factors in criminal records, evictions, and several other factors to provide a better predictor of a potential tenant's ability to pay rent.

APPROVAL REQUIREMENTS

We use the following chart to bring the two components together (Income-to-Rent Ratio and NTN Score) to evaluate every application.

Status	NTN Score	Income-to-Rent Ratio
Approved	85 or above	3.0 or above
Conditional	65 to 84	3.0 or above
Declined	64 or below	N/A

Approval—These applicants are automatically approved and generally are the best tenants. Once we have an applicant that is approved, we move quickly to get a lease signed and deposits collected.

Conditional—These applicants can be approved or declined. Generally, we dig a little deeper to understand why their NTN Score is below 85 and then make a decision to accept or decline these applicants.

Declined—These applicants are automatically declined, no matter what their Income-to-Rent Ratio is, as a result of their poor NTN Score.

If you are using an online application process that uses only a credit score, you would create an acceptance criteria as follows:

Status	Credit Score	Income-to-Rent Ratio
Approved	680 or above	3.0 or above
Conditional	600 to 679	3.0 or above
Declined	599 or below	N/A

As I mentioned, the Income-to-Rent Ratio and NTN Score are our primary tools to approve or decline an applicant. There are, however, some additional criteria that can influence your decision to accept or decline someone.

Exclusion of Medical Bills

One exclusion you can make when implementing your approval process is with medical bills. For example, a prospective tenant may have gotten into a bad car accident a few years ago and been unable to pay the costs associated with their treatment, care, and recovery. That should not exclude them from being able to rent an apartment. NTN's system allows us to exclude medical bills from counting against a prospective tenant.

PERMITTED NUMBER OF PEOPLE

Most local cities or townships will have housing rules or regulations that limit the number of people who can live in a house or apartment to prevent overcrowding. You might have a tenant who approaches you for an apartment, and they have a strong NTN Score and an acceptable Income-to-Rent Ratio. However, if they have six children and your apartment is a two-bedroom unit, it will likely not be in compliance with your local housing requirements. Accepting them may result in fines or penalties from your local housing authority.

Most municipalities, as a general rule, will allow two people per bedroom, but there is some variance by local or state regulations.

SMOKING OR NONSMOKING?

Just like you need to have a pet policy, every landlord should also have a smoking policy. Smokers are not a protected class under HUD's Fair Housing rules, and landlords have the option to accept or decline an applicant based on their smoking status.

Currently, about 12% of Americans smoke. So not accepting a smoker will not have a huge impact on your potential tenants, like pet owners, which are over 65% of Americans. Whether to allow smoking or not comes down to a decision on opening up your apartments to the shrinking minority of smokers left in the world or renting exclusively to nonsmokers.

You must remember to be up front in your advertising. Put either "Smokers OK" or "No Smoking" in your advertisements. This will save you and the applicant the time and effort of showing the apartment in case they fall into the wrong category.

There is also the option to charge a slightly higher rent to a person that smokes and improve your return on your investment. We at Del Val are not currently doing this but have considered charging an extra 5% or 10% rent for smokers.

If you are renting to someone in a multiunit building, you need to consider secondhand smoke and how it may affect other tenants. Some people think that as long as smoking is confined to an apartment, it will not bother the other tenants. But this is not true. Smoke seeps into the walls and through the windows and doorways; it gets into the air of common areas and can be a serious turn-off to nonsmokers, as well as a detriment to their health.

COSIGNERS OR FINANCIAL GUARANTORS?

If you run into a situation where the prospective tenant is young and has no credit history, you might ask for a cosigner or financial guarantor, usually a parent or legal guardian. Until recently, attorneys were advising to ask for cosigners. Today, however, more attorneys are suggesting the use of financial guarantors.

The difference between the two terms is that a cosigner signs the lease. A financial guarantor does not; they sign a separate document guaranteeing the rent payment. This means a financial guarantor would not appear in court during eviction procedures. If the judge rules in your favor for a valid eviction of the tenant, you may then ask (demand) the financial guarantor for payment. This may require you to appear in court a second time if the financial guarantor does not cover the unpaid rent and legal costs to evict the tenant.

A big question arises when it comes to weak applicants with cosigners or financial guarantors. Should you accept them? For example, college students have notoriously bad or insufficient credit. You might have a student applicant with an NTN Score of 58 and a borderline Income-to-Rent Ratio. If they have a parent willing to cosign or act as a financial guarantor with an NTN Score of 95, the average of the two would put them in the conditional zone and could be accepted or declined according to our system.

MULTIPLE TENANTS

Not all applicants are simple to accept or deny. As a landlord, you will encounter married couples with or without kids, roommates, and even sublets or assignments. For many landlords, these situations can be confusing to navigate, but you will know exactly how to handle each of them after reading the following paragraphs.

COTENANTS

Couples and roommates can come to whatever agreement they want for rent payments, but the total rent must be paid every month. All tenants are jointly responsible for the rent and utility payments.

We included the following statement on the first page of our lease to make it clear that all tenants are jointly liable for the lease and all payments or any damages (see Appendix A).

> If more than one resident signs this lease, each Resident is responsible individually and together for the full rent payment and all other utilities and fees. For example, if one Resident moves out, the Landlord can make the remaining Residents responsible for paying the full rent and utilities. It also means the Landlord can sue either Resident for breaking the Lease.

Remember what I said earlier, which is worth repeating: *everyone living in the apartment and over the age of eighteen must complete an application and sign the lease.* If the total rent is $1,500 and two tenants pay you $500 and the third does not pay, all three tenants are responsible for the remaining unpaid rent. All three tenants are also responsible for late fees and potentially eviction if the total rent remains unpaid.

ADDING PEOPLE TO THE LEASE

Another situation you may encounter is when a tenant has a guest staying for the foreseeable future. You may even have a tenant that brings someone in to help with the rent payments.

Regardless of the arrangement, if someone is living in your apartment for more than thirty days their name should be added to the lease. This does not happen often, but when it does, you want to charge a fee of $250 to $500 to complete the new paperwork and begin the approval process for the new tenant.

SUBLETTING

Another thing that does not happen often, but might if you own enough residential rental units, is that you might encounter a tenant who wants to sublet their apartment. Our sample lease (Appendix A) does not allow subletting.

If a tenant approaches you and asks to sublet the unit, you have the option to negotiate. You can collect a fee of $250 to $500 to process the paperwork and allow the sublet if they meet your approval criteria discussed above. But to keep it simple, I recommend sticking with the "no sublets" clause in the sample lease provided.

ASSIGNMENTS

Another situation that may come up from time to time is assignments. These happen when your current tenant tells you that they are moving out, but they have a friend, coworker, or other acquaintance who wants to rent the apartment.

Again, the recommended option is to stick with the sample lease and tell the tenant that no assignments are allowed, but their friend is more than welcome to fill out an application after the apartment has been cleaned and advertised as vacant.

If you decide to allow assignments I recommend charging $250 to $500 for processing the paperwork.

STICK WITH IT

The most important thing to remember about the application and approval process is to stay firmly within your system. Do not round up or down on the NTN Score or the Income-to-Rent Ratio to include or exclude potential tenants. When it comes to your approval system, *stick with it.*

In the next chapter, you will learn whether you should consider allowing pets. Some of the answers may surprise you.

CHAPTER 6

SHOULD YOU ALLOW PETS?

A recent study by the American Pet Products Association states that 68% of US households own pets; yet only 55% of landlords allow pets in their rental properties.[17] From my observations, pet ownership in single-family homes is becoming more popular over the last few years and may well be above the 68% figure. If you own single-family homes and do not allow pets, you are eliminating three quarters of your potential tenants. This means it could take extra weeks, or even months, to get your property rented, losing thousands of dollars in profit over that time frame.

As a landlord, the profitability of considering pets may seem counterintuitive. You might think about puppies chewing on crown molding, cats scratching everything in sight, and even menacing-looking animals posing a threat to other tenants or neighbors. These are legitimate concerns when renting to tenants with pets, but my experience has shown that the pros outweigh the cons in the vast majority of cases.

---

[17] American Humane, "Pet-Friendly Tips for Landlords," accessed October 9, 2023, https://www.americanhumane.org/fact-sheet/pet-friendly-tips-for-landlords/.

Pets are *not* a protected class under The Fair Housing Act (FHA), which prevents discrimination against tenants. As a landlord, you are fully within your rights to accept or decline tenants with pets.

Again, this book is about maximizing profits. Accepting pets is a big opportunity to get more income from your rental properties. Still, there are advantages and disadvantages that must be considered before you can make a truly informed decision.

ADVANTAGES OF A PRO-PETS POLICY

If you choose to accept pets it must be done correctly and must be a part of your written lease and application process. You must also define what pets you might be willing to accept, and which pets you want to exclude. With the understanding that you want to maximize profits, let us first discuss the advantages of accepting pets.

A LARGER POPULATION CAN RENT YOUR PROPERTY

According to an Apartments.com survey, over 60% of renters who have pets claim to have a hard time finding an apartment that will accept pets.[18] This has become a national issue, and the shortage of apartments that accept pets is getting worse as pets become more popular. As a landlord, you have an opportunity to help this situation and make extra money.

INCREASED RENEWALS

Another reason you should at least consider allowing pets in your

---

[18] Chad Garland, "More than 70% of Apartment Renters Own Pets, Survey Finds," *Los Angeles Times*, August 12, 2014, https://www.latimes.com/business/la-fi-survey-renters-pet-friendly-options-20140811-story.html.

rental properties is that pet owners tend to stay longer than other tenants. A study by the Foundation for Interdisciplinary Research and Education Promoting Animal Welfare (FIREPAW) shows that pet owners stayed an average of twenty-three months versus fifteen months for non–pet owners.[19] If you are a pet owner, it is very hard to move, so they tend to renew leases and stay longer. Less turnover means no vacancy in between tenants, no cleaning or painting between tenants, or repairing any damage between tenants. This is a huge cost saving.

PET OWNERS TEND TO HAVE HIGHER INCOMES

Another advantage is that pet owners tend to have higher incomes. Feeding and caring for a dog or a cat costs a significant amount of money. The average pet owner spends between $100 and $250 per month in food, toys, health care visits, and other associated costs. People with higher incomes tend to make better tenants who can afford setbacks in their lives without missing their rent payments.

MAKE MORE MONEY

Perhaps the biggest advantage of allowing pets is more money through a premium rent. If an apartment is worth $1,500 per month, you might be able to ask $1,600, or even $1,700, because pet-friendly units may be scarce in your area.

Additionally, our standard pet agreements also allow you to charge an extra $40 to $60 per month for each pet. At Del Val, we also charge a pet security of $300 for each pet.

---

[19] Pamela Carlisle-Frank, Joshua M. Frank, and Lindsey Nielsen, "Companion Animal Renters and Pet-Friendly Housing in the US," *Anthrozoös* 18, no. 1 (2005): 59–77, https://doi.org/10.2752/089279305785594270.

A pro-pet policy is one of the easier ways to maximize profits. If you charge an extra $100 per month as premium rent and $50 per month per pet, that is $1,800 more per year in income from just one rental unit. The FIREPAW study estimates that on average a pet generates an extra $2,731 per unit per year.[20]

Now, think back to a previous chapter when I talked about how your building's value equates to approximately one hundred times the monthly rent. The increased rent of $150 per month means the value of your property will increase by approximately $15,000 ($150 × 100). What if you own ten buildings? That means an extra $150,000 in property value just by allowing pets.

DISADVANTAGES OF A PRO-PETS POLICY

It should now be clear that allowing pets is a great way to maximize profits as a landlord. I would be remiss, however, if I did not mention the caveats that come with a pro-pets policy. There are disadvantages you should at least be aware of before making your decision on whether or not to allow pets in your rental units.

PROPERTY DAMAGE

The first thing is the possibility that pets can cause damage to your property. In the FIREPAW study, 85% of landlords who accepted pets reported having pet-related damage at some point during their time as a landlord.[21] But in most cases, the cost of the damage was

---

[20] Carlisle-Frank, Frank, and Nielsen, "Companion Animal Renters."

[21] Carlisle-Frank, Frank, and Nielsen, "Companion Animal Renters."

covered by the required pet security deposit, and the landlord did not have any substantial monetary losses.

The FIREPAW study also showed that the total difference in property damage from landlords with pets and landlords without pets was under $40, with an average of $323 in damages for tenants without pets and an average of $362 for tenants with pets.[22] This is hardly enough to give up thousands of dollars in extra rent per year.

LIABILITY

Another reason you may choose not to allow pets—in particular, dogs—is the concern they might injure someone, which might require you to spend a lot of legal money defending yourself in court. This situation, however, is not as likely as it may seem.

It is rare that a landlord is found to be liable for injuries inflicted by their tenant's dog. Just the fact that you have rented out your property to a tenant is not enough for a landlord to be found responsible for injuries caused by a dog.

The general rule is that landlords will only be found guilty if either of the following are true:

- The landlord knew the dog was dangerous and could have had the dog removed.
- The landlord "harbored" or "kept" the tenant's dog, meaning they cared for it or had some control over the dog.

---

[22] Carlisle-Frank, Frank, and Nielsen, "Companion Animal Renters."

As long as you are not directly involved in the care of a dog, or if you become aware the dog may be dangerous and do not put the tenant on notice of the dog's danger, you should be fine.

In the rare event a landlord is found responsible for a dog's harm, a landlord's owner's liability insurance may cover the loss.

NOISE AND MULTIUNIT BUILDINGS

Accepting pets in multiunit buildings is a little tricky. As a general rule, we do not permit pets in multiunit buildings. The reason is noise and tenants' complaints. For example, the sound of a neighbor's door opening when they come home from work late at night is often enough to trigger a dog in a nearby apartment to start barking. This obviously creates a disturbance for all the tenants.

One solution is to make the entire building pet and dog friendly and make it very clear to all applicants that there will be dogs in the building. The other option would be to accept all pets except dogs.

An Important Note about Service and Emotional Support Animals

Keep in mind that Service Dogs (SD) and Emotional Support Animals (ESA) are *not* considered pets, and pet rules and restrictions do not apply. ESAs help people with emotional disabilities such as anxiety or depression by providing comfort and support.

Any animal can be an ESA. Federal law does not require these animals to have any specific training, and the owner of an ESA does not have to be physically disabled, whereas SDs *do* require special training.

In most cases, your tenant(s) should provide a letter from their doctor stating that they have a disability that benefits from an SD or ESA. Tenants asking for accommodations for their ESA can be asked to provide a letter from their therapist or mental health care provider.

Landlords also need to understand the difference between service animals, therapy animals, and emotional support animals. The below chart will help with the features and permissions for each type of animal.

COMPARISON	SERVICE DOGS	THERAPY DOGS	SUPPORT ANIMALS
ADA Covered: right to bring animal into public establishments	✓	✗	✗
Needs to tolerate a wide variety of experiences, environments, and people	✓	✓	✗
May live with their disabled owners even if "no pets" policy in place	✓	✗	✓
Primary functions is to provide emotional support through companionship	✗	✗	✓
Specifically trained to assist just one person	✓	✗	✗
Provides emotional support and comfort to many people	✗	✓	✗

PRECAUTIONS TO TAKE WHEN ALLOWING PETS

If you weigh the advantages and disadvantages of allowing pets and come to the conclusion that being pet friendly in your rental units is worth the risk, there are some precautions of which you should be aware.

PET APPLICATIONS

As we discussed, accepting pets can be very profitable, but you must put in certain precautions. The first precaution is to require a pet application. We use a service called PetScreening.com.

Our applicants go to this website and fill in all the information regarding the dog, cat, or other animals they want to have in their rental unit. The site will ask them a series of questions, like what type of animal it is, the breed, the size and weight, the shots they have had, and some other details.

When the prospective tenant is done filling out the screening request, the website rates the pet's viability as an acceptable risk on a scale from one to five "Paws." A rating of one Paw means the pet would bring a high (potentially unacceptable) amount of risk to your property. A rating of five Paws means the pet adds little risk to the property owner. We also charge a higher pet rent for Paws scores of one or two and less pet rent for four or five Paws.

PetScreening.com offers additional resources that may help you as a landlord as well. For instance, they can verify assistance animals per HUD and FHA guidelines. They also have some great documentation and FAQs that you may find helpful.

DOG BREEDS (AND MORE) TO AVOID

Certain dog breeds have a history of being more problematic than others, especially when it comes to human safety and legal issues. Some types of dogs are labeled as aggressive by property insurance providers and should not be permitted on the property regardless of your pet policy. Here is a list of breeds you may want to exclude from your rental units:

- Akita
- Malamute
- American Bull Terrier/American Bulldog
- American Staffordshire Terrier
- Chow Chow
- Coyotes/Wild dogs
- Doberman Pinscher
- German Shepherd
- Hybrid and purebred wolves
- Korean Jindo
- Pit Bull
- Presa Canario
- Rottweiler
- Husky
- Staffordshire Bull Terrier
- Plus reptiles, snakes, or exotic animals of any sort

Most property insurance providers may void any policy of a landlord who rents to someone with one of the above breeds. So it is my recommendation to adhere to this list and consult your insurance advisor on what breeds may not be permitted.

NUMBER OF PETS

While most tenants do not have more than one or two pets, we recommend establishing a limit that makes sense for the size of the property you own. If somebody wants to rent your picturesque single-family ranch home and they tell you that they have six or eight cats, you probably want to rule that person out. Similarly, if they want to rent your 500-square-foot apartment and they have two ninety-pound rottweilers, they might not be the best fit for that particular unit. You also need to ensure you follow city laws regarding how many animals you are allowed to have in a residential property or apartment.

WEIGHT OF DOGS

I recommend putting a weight limit on pets of around forty to fifty pounds. Any dog bigger than that can cause significant damage and scare off a lot of other quality tenants.

CONDO OR HOMEOWNERS ASSOCIATIONS

If your property is inside a condo or homeowners association, they may have their own pet rules typically dealing with permitted breeds and weight limits. I would recommend calling your condo or HOA manager and getting a copy of the pet rules so you can be sure to stay compliant.

PETS ADDENDUM WITH RULES AND REGULATIONS

As part of our standard lease, we require all tenants to sign a Pet Addendum with exactly what we expect from the pet owner and the penalties for not complying with the pet rules. If they fail to comply with our Pet Addendum, we could declare a material breach of the lease and potentially remove the tenant from the property through a legal eviction process.

A FINAL WORD ON PETS

After having all that information in hand, it is up to you to decide whether or not you should rent to someone with pets. Is the potential for maximized profits worth the risk of damage or disturbances? The final call is yours to make.

In the next chapter, you will learn the tips and strategies on how to prepare a lease that protects the landlord, not the tenant.

CHAPTER 7

HOW TO PREPARE A LEASE THAT PROTECTS THE LANDLORD AND GENERATES EXTRA FEES

ost sample leases that can be downloaded from the Internet are designed with the tenant's best interest in mind. Although they fulfill the basic requirements to get a tenant in your apartment and pay rent, they restrict your flexibility and leave you vulnerable as a landlord. Furthermore, these documents will hinder your ability to maximize profits.

I also see some landlords use nothing but a verbal agreement. This gives the tenant all the control. *The lease in Appendix A is written with specific clauses that protect you, the landlord, not the tenant.* It is perhaps the most valuable piece of information you can take from this book.

By saying the lease protects the landlord, not the tenant, I am not—in any way—suggesting that it contains anything dishonest or disreputable. Although our lease is nuanced in comparison to those you will find online, it is fair and transparent. Still, you should disclose anything to your prospective tenants that could raise questions. If they have any question you cannot answer, you should advise them to seek legal counsel to fully explain the lease and their obligations.

Is a Rental Agreement Different from a Lease?

There is one big difference between a lease and a rental agreement. A lease has a fixed term attached to it, typically one or two years. It will contain exact dates for a beginning and an end date. A rental agreement, however, is usually a thirty-day contract that automatically rolls over until the tenant or landlord formally terminates the contract.

Rental agreements are also called "short-term property contracts." They are mostly used in boardinghouses and temporary housing typically for thirty, sixty, or ninety days. Unless you are operating a boardinghouse, I would suggest you use a lease.

LEASE ESSENTIALS

As stated in Chapter 5, *everyone living in your apartment who is over the age of eighteen must sign the lease.* This is critical that all persons over eighteen actually sign the lease so you have a complete lease.

You will undoubtedly run into situations where tenants want an exception to this rule. Someone may have a nineteen-year-old child in college who just stays with them for the summers; they need to be on the lease. Another tenant may say that their elderly grandparent is living with them temporarily until they find a suitable place for them to live; they need to be on the lease. Still another tenant may have someone who is "between living situations" and needs a place to "crash" for a while. Everyone has a different story, but stick to your lease policies and have all occupants over eighteen sign the lease.

Your rule of thumb should be that if anyone is living in the apartment for more than thirty days, they need to sign the lease. If there are children under the age of eighteen, they should be listed under a section titled "Additional Occupants," but they do not actually sign the lease. Much like the approval process, if you stick with the rules of the legally binding agreement, you will avoid headaches in the future.

TERM LENGTH

Your standard lease should be for a fixed term of one or two years. Most tenants will prefer a one-year agreement because it allows them the flexibility to move without paying a penalty for early termination. This flexibility can also work in your favor as it provides an opportunity to raise the rent at the end of the first year. One-year leases are another way to maximize profits.

If you elect to use two years as your standard lease agreement, that can also work in your favor. A longer term means locked-in business for an extended period of time. That peace of mind in knowing that you will have rent coming in for the next twenty-four months is valuable to a lot of landlords.

Weigh the benefits of flexibility versus extended guaranteed income to decide whether you prefer a one- or two-year lease.

Occasionally, someone may want to rent your apartment for only six, eight, or nine months. They could be building a house and want a place to live until it is completed. Perhaps they are temporarily relocating for a business venture. There are a number of reasons that a tenant might want this sort of arrangement. If it happens, I encourage you not to dismiss the idea. A shorter term means a premium of anywhere from 10% to 25% on your monthly rent. You decide what an appropriate increase looks like and see if the potential tenant agrees.

Our lease stipulates that the tenant is required to give sixty days' notice if they plan to move out at the end of the lease term. Otherwise, our lease automatically rolls over into a month-to-month agreement with an automatic 10% increase in the monthly rent.

The 10% increase is basically a fee for the tenant to have the flexibility to move out with just a thirty-day notice. It can be used as a bargaining chip to encourage the tenant to sign a new long-term lease. For example, your tenant might agree to sign a new one-year lease with only a 4% increase, but you now have an occupied unit for the next twelve months.

DUE DATE

Your lease should clearly state when the rent is due. Consistency is key here if you own multiple properties. You want to keep things as simple as possible by having a due date for rent on the same day of every month for every unit. Unpaid rent and late fees become easier to track when clear due dates are established and maintained across your property portfolio.

Whatever due date you choose, make sure it is clearly spelled out in the lease, along with the exact day that a late fee will be added.

UTILITIES

Because our lease is written to protect the landlord, it simply states that tenants are responsible for *all* utilities. This is another way that our lease is different from standard documents you will find on the Internet. Most leases have a series of checkboxes next to water, electricity, gas, cable, etc. We do not do that at Del Val but simply state the tenant is responsible for all utilities.

The only deviation we have to the above is the water bill in a multi-tenant dwelling where there is only one water meter. In this case, the lease spells out a fixed amount per month for water.

PESTS

Our pest policy at Del Val stipulates that if a tenant has any pest issues within the first thirty days of occupancy, it is our responsibility to treat them and we will cover any associated costs. Anything after that is the tenant's responsibility. The assumption is that if rodents or pests are noticed in the first thirty days, they may have been there before the tenant moved in. Thus, we should pay to get rid of the pests. If rodents or pests are discovered after the tenant has lived in the apartment for thirty days, it is likely they are doing something to attract the pests and it is their responsibility to remove them.

RENTER'S INSURANCE

Many landlords leave renter's insurance up to the tenant's discretion. Our lease states that the tenant *must* have renter's insurance. In fact, make sure you get a copy of their policy to keep on file in case you need it in the future.

When the tenant has renter's insurance, any damage they suffer to their belongings, such as televisions, furniture, clothing, etc. will be covered. Additionally, renter's insurance will cover any damage to their car while parked.

ADDENDUMS

There are a number of addendums attached to our sample lease in Appendix A that cover the following sections:

- Rules and regulations
- Drug-free housing
- Pets
- Lead paint
- Security deposit refund
- Bed bugs
- Mold

The addendums listed above are fairly basic and should be included in most leases. There may be some states that require additional addendums. Consult with a real estate attorney to find out which of these addendums you need to add to your lease.

ELECTRONIC SIGNATURES

In the past, landlords would discuss lease terms with their tenants in a local coffee shop or in their offices, and this could take hours to complete. But today, you can send the lease to your tenant via email with an e-signature software program. The software we use is called DocuSign. However, there are a number of other similar software programs that perform the same function. One of the best features of DocuSign is once all parties have signed the lease, each party receives a pdf version of the signed document.

Despite the ease of using e-signatures software, it is still important that your prospective tenants can ask questions and get clarification on specific parts of your lease. I would make sure your tenants can email or call if they have questions.

WHY TENANTS PREFER ELECTRONIC SIGNATURES

Most tenants appreciate the convenience of e-signatures. There is no need to meet with them for an hour to go over every page in detail. It is also possible to save a pdf of the signed lease if they lose the printed version.

WHY LANDLORDS PREFER ELECTRONIC SIGNATURES

Landlords appreciate the same convenience factor that electronic signatures provide. You can create a template of your lease and send the same lease to every new tenant to sign. Some tenants may have cosigners or financial guarantors who live far away. E-signatures allow them to sign the document with no travel required for you or the cosigner.

Another benefit for using software to sign your leases is that you do not need to keep paper records. This can be especially helpful if you own multiple properties and have accumulated many signed leases over the years. Rather than a bulging folder full of old lease paperwork, you can simply have everything stored on your computer.

Using electronic signature software is also an indicator of professionalism. As a landlord, this tells the tenant that you are aware of modern technology, which also shows them that you are likely to ensure their apartment is up to today's living standards.

EXTRA FEES

One of the keys to maximize your revenue as a landlord is to charge tenants if they are not complying with your lease. There are a variety of extra fees that should be written into your lease agreement if the tenant violates any of the lease terms. If you use the sample lease provided in Appendix A, you will see this lease charges for late fees, notice to quit fees, non-sufficient funds, holdover fees, unauthorized pet fees, and lost keys.

LATE FEES

Throughout your years as a landlord, you will run into different types of tenants. One of the most common is the constant negotiator. This is the person who approaches you with something like, "Hey, can I pay you $500 now and another $500 in two weeks?" Generally, we will allow this payment plan, but the late fee is nonnegotiable. Our lease charges a flat $75 late fee if the rent is outstanding on the fifth of the month and is greater than $300.

You should give your tenants a few days as a grace period before charging a late fee. I would recommend no more than five to ten days. If your due date is the first of the month, a late fee should kick in on the fifth or tenth depending on how many days you allow as a grace period. That gives your tenants a full five days after the due date to come up with the unpaid balance.

We allow an outstanding balance of up to $300 before we charge a late fee. This avoids charging late fees for small balances.

You can adjust this amount to fit your landlord business, but we feel this is a good compromise between being firm as a landlord and allowing the tenant a little wiggle room.

There are a number of ways you can charge late fees.

- You can charge a daily fee for every day the rent is late such as $5.00 to $10.00 per day for any outstanding rent over $300. This is not recommended because judges do not typically like daily fees and it becomes difficult to track.
- You can charge a percentage of the rent, such as 5% to 10% at the end of the grace period.
- You can charge a fixed amount at the end of the grace period, such as $50 to $250.
- You could also use a combination of any of the above.

Keep in mind that if you charge a late fee and have to evict your tenant, you need to show your late fee is "reasonable." What is reasonable may change from court to court, but if your late fee is 10% of the rent or less, most judges would accept that charge as reasonable. If your late fee is 25% or more, it may be determined "unreasonable," and you will not be awarded that money in your eviction hearing case.

Our view has always been that the flat fee is the best charge for late rent. We feel that the daily fee is administratively difficult. If the tenant has a prolonged period of outstanding rent, it can quickly accumulate to a point where it becomes out of control and not "reasonable." At Del Val, we charge $75 if a tenant does not pay the rent by the end of business on the fifth of the month and has an outstanding balance of over $300. We feel this is a simple strategy and has never been thrown out by a judge.

Understanding that $75 is a lot more to a tenant who is only paying $600 for rent than it is to someone paying $2,500 per month, you could opt for a percentage structure for late fees. If you go this route I would not go above 10% as discussed above.

If you own several properties with a wide spectrum of rents, from low to high, you could invoke a tiered system for late fees. For example, the late fee for apartments with rents under $1,000 could be $75; for apartments between $1,000 and $2,000, the fee could be $100; anything over $2,000 could be $150 to $200. You decide the exact structure.

According to Avail, over 80% of rental leases include late fees, but only 12% of landlords actually enforce them.[23] Part of being a professional landlord includes charging and *enforcing* your late fees.

NOTICE TO QUIT

When a tenant is late on rent for an extended period of time, or chronically late, you might need to start an eviction process. It is up to you how long to wait before proceeding with an eviction, but in the state of Pennsylvania, the start of the legal process involves sending the tenant a legal letter called a "Notice to Quit."

Each state may differ in their eviction processes and might call this letter something different, but most likely all states require you

[23] Kasia Manolas, "Late Rent Fees and Grace Periods," Avail, Realtor.com, last modified August 19, 2022, https://www.avail.co/education/guides/complete-guide-to-rent-collection/late-rent-fees-and-grace-periods#.

to put the tenant on notice that they are in violation of their lease and legal action may be started unless they cure the violation. Our lease agreement allows us to charge the tenant $25 for mailing and posting the Notice to Quit on the front door.

One way our sample lease protects you—the landlord—is that it contains a waiver of the "Notice to Quit" document. This is 100% legal and allows you to begin eviction proceedings immediately following nonpayment or some other violation of the lease. Although you would not want to invoke an eviction the first time a tenant is late with their rent, this waiver allows you to do so and gives you the upper hand as a landlord.

NON-SUFFICIENT FUNDS (NSF)

In the event that a check you accept fails to clear, you are entitled to charge a fee. Checks that do not clear due to insufficient funds (NSF) should be charged $25 to $75.

HOLDOVER FEES

In most situations, a departing tenant should schedule their move-out for the end of the month. If they provide notice that they would leave your property by March 31, but their moving truck cannot get there until April 3, they are subject to a holdover fee.

Our sample lease includes a holdover fee of $50 per day plus 150% of their normal rent. This might seem steep, but the tenant is delaying your ability to get your unit ready and find a new tenant. You cannot do anything to prepare the unit until it is unoccupied. It is perfectly reasonable to have that tenant pay for your lost time and money.

UNAUTHORIZED PETS

We covered this fee in the chapter on pets. For now, understand that tenants need to tell you if a pet is living at the property. At Del Val, we ask for $40 to $60 per month, depending on the type of pet and the size. If you discover an unauthorized pet in one of your units, we recommend a fee of $250 to $500 plus your normal pet rent per month going forward.

LOST KEYS

Another additional fee that landlords run into with fair regularity is for lost keys. Some tenants are prone to losing keys. There is a cost to making additional keys and delivering. A lost key fee should be somewhere between $75 and $150. This is another reason to consider smart locks as they do not have keys, as discussed in Chapter 2.

HOW TO ALLOCATE MONIES RECEIVED

This is one of the most important sections of your lease; it lists the sequence of accounts where money received will be assigned. For example, suppose a tenant is $500 behind on their rent and you have added a late fee of $100, creating a total unpaid balance of $600. Where does the money go when the tenant sends you $500? Does it all go to the rent? Or does $400 go to the rent and $100 to the late fee, leaving them $100 short on rent?

Any money received from a tenant should go to everything else before it is applied to current rent. The order by which you should allocate funds is as follows:

1. Late rent, returned checks, and Notice to Quit fees
2. Legal and/or court fees
3. Utility bills (if applicable)
4. Past rent
5. Current rent

If you were to start an eviction and tell the judge that the tenant is $100 behind on unpaid late fees, the judge will not remove the tenant for that. They will tell you to work it out with the tenant and come back if no resolution has been reached.

As a rule, judges do not want to evict tenants. There is a homelessness crisis in America, and judges are not going to put people on the street for late fees. Unpaid rent, however, is a different situation. A judge cannot allow a tenant to live in your apartment for free.

If you go to court and tell the judge that the tenant is behind on rent, they have no wiggle room. At that point, the judge will take action to make sure you get paid or the tenant gets removed. For this reason, current rent is always the last allocation of money received.

Whether you use our sample lease, create your own, or use another online option, make sure that the order of payment is plainly written for the tenant and any potential legal authority to see.

A FINAL WORD ON PREPARING A LEASE

As you now have an understanding of how a lease protects a landlord's interest and generates extra fees, it is time to discuss security deposits.

CHAPTER 8

SECURITY DEPOSIT SECRETS

Many landlords underestimate the importance of managing security deposits. They collect the funds, throw them into their operating account, and forget about them until the tenant moves out. But security deposits are an area where landlords make mistakes that can get you in trouble with state regulators.

Security deposits are the tenant's money that is held in escrow by the landlord in case a tenant causes damages or defaults on their lease. State regulators and attorney generals pay special attention to security deposits and possible mismanagement of these funds because landlords are holding the money on behalf of the tenants. Government officials have a duty to protect the tenant's interests. I am not saying this to frighten you, but to be sure, you must be aware how to treat these monies to stay compliant with your state regulations.

Each state has rules on how much security you can collect. For example, Pennsylvania allows landlords to collect two months of security at the beginning of the lease, but only one month after one year of tenancy. New Jersey caps security deposits at one-and-a-half month's worth of rent. California is currently passing a law to minimize a security deposit to one month. Some states have no limits but all the states have rules on how these monies are handled.

In some states, if you raise the rent, you are not allowed to increase the security deposit amounts. Other states have limits regarding people who are over sixty-two years old. Different parts of the country will also dictate various laws for furnished versus unfurnished units. So know your state rules!

Know Your State's Laws

For a breakdown of security deposit laws by state, please see: https://www.rocketlawyer.com/real-estate/landlords/property-management/legal-guide/security-deposit-laws-by-state.

SECURITY DEPOSIT VERSUS LAST MONTH'S RENT

There is a lot of controversy about whether a "last month" is the same as a security deposit. A lot of landlords like to collect the first and last month and one month of security. If the tenant defaults, they use the "last month" to offset some of the damages. It is not always clear if this is legally acceptable.

I speak from experience in this matter. Many years ago, Del Val allowed the last month of rent to serve as a tenant's security deposit. When we had to go to court for nonpayment issues, the judge got confused and would not allow us to use the "last month" to offset unpaid rent.

Our solution has been to charge the tenant upon move-in for the first month's rent and two months' security deposit. This way it is clear that we are holding security deposit funds that can be used to offset any damages or unpaid rent.

HOW TO HANDLE SECURITY DEPOSITS

When a tenant signs the initial lease and provides you with a security deposit, you must keep this money in a separate "escrow" account. You cannot mix security funds in your operating or personal accounts (see Chapter 14).

A checking or savings account labeled "Security Deposit Escrow" would meet this requirement and is clear for any state regulators. But it is critical to never use the security deposit for anything other than a lease default. These funds can never be used for general operating expenses. In some states, you must also give any interest earned on the security deposit to the tenant at move-out. In Pennsylvania, landlords are allowed to keep the first 1% of interest and all interest over that must be given to the tenants.

When a tenant moves out and you need to retain some, or all, of a tenant's security deposit, you must send a letter outlining all the damages and the cost to repair those items and any unpaid rent. If the damages do not exceed the total security, you would then return what is remaining from their security deposit.

You must return these funds within a specific number of days, according to state law. Pennsylvania requires a landlord to return the security deposits within thirty days. In some states, if you fail to return the security deposit in a timely manner, you might owe the tenant double the amount of their security deposit. This is a particularly harsh lesson to learn and a good example of why properly managing security deposits is a critical item on your list of landlord responsibilities.

VALID REASONS TO KEEP MONEY FROM A SECURITY DEPOSIT

Different states have varying rules that declare when a landlord can hold onto a security deposit and for how long. Theoretically, you—the landlord—can withhold a security deposit for the following reasons:

1. To repair damages considered beyond "normal wear and tear"
2. To clean the unit if it is left excessively dirty
3. To cover a tenant's default on any unpaid rent or fees
4. To cover any unpaid utility bills that are required to be paid by the tenant

You might be asking, "What is 'normal wear and tear'?" If a tenant lives in an apartment for two or three years, there are going to be small holes in the walls from hanging pictures and other items. The rugs are going to be slightly worn and some dirt and dust will gather under the sinks and in the kitchen cabinets. You cannot keep a tenant's security deposit for these items, as they fall under the umbrella term "normal wear and tear."

DAMAGE

A broken window is a different story. Also, small holes in the wall from hanging pictures are expected, but larger, gaping spaces from someone's anger-fueled fist or a thrown object are not acceptable. A slightly worn carpet is fine, but permanent stains or burn marks are not. If a situation such as a leak goes unreported long enough to cause damage to the ceiling, drywall, flooring, or carpet, that is another instance where a security deposit could be used for repairs or replacements.

CLEANING

Keeping the security deposit to *clean* the apartment is a gray area. If the tenant has not bothered to clean the bathroom or kitchen for three years, you might be justified in using their money to pay for the cleaning. The term used by property managers and landlords is "broom clean." Unfortunately, broom clean is not clearly defined.

UNPAID RENT OR FEES

Additionally, if the tenant owes you money for unpaid rent or fees, you can keep the security deposit to offset these unpaid charges. This includes any of the fees mentioned in the previous chapters, including pets, late fees, holdover fees, and others.

UTILITY BILLS

As long as the tenant was required to pay for the utility costs in your lease, you can also use security funds to offset unpaid utility bills.

A LIST OF REQUIREMENTS FOR TENANTS TO COLLECT THE SECURITY DEPOSIT

One of the addendums in Appendix A acts as a road map for the tenant to get their security deposit back. A tenant should read this prior to moving out if they want to get their security back. You can also resend it to your tenants, if they have provided a notice to move out, as a reminder of how to get their security deposit back.

The following list summarizes the requirements from that page of the sample lease:

1. A written sixty-day (or whatever you require) Notice to Vacate must be provided to the landlord. If you do not give the full sixty-day notice before the lease termination date, the lease will automatically renew on a month-to-month basis and notice must be given thirty days prior to the end of the month of the lease extension.

2. All rent and/or charges must be paid in full.

3. All keys must be returned to the landlord. Rent will be charged until all keys are returned or the unit is returned to the landlord through the courts.

4. Your apartment must be left in a clean condition. You must clean the stove, exhaust and range hood, refrigerator, all other appliances, bathroom fixtures, and cabinets. Tenants must also remove all trash and personal items.

5. You will be charged for damage beyond normal wear and tear to the apartment. This includes missing items such as light bulbs, drip pans, toilet paper holders, screens, doorknobs, etc.

6. A forwarding address must be given at the time of move-out. Failure to supply the landlord with a forwarding address at the time of move-out may result in your security deposit not being sent in a timely manner.

7. In the case of eviction, the tenant automatically forfeits their entire security deposit and will be billed for all necessary painting and cleaning damages beyond normal wear and tear, keys not returned, etc.

SECURITY DEPOSIT ALTERNATIVES

A harsh reality exists in that most renters do not have enough money saved to pay the first month's rent plus two months' security deposit. In fact, 60% of American workers live paycheck to paycheck.[24]

A tenant moving into an apartment that rents for $2,000 per month must have $6,000 at move-in as a security deposit along with the first month's rent. And this does not include moving expenses and the cost to set up cable/Internet. These large up-front expenses present a challenge for many potential applicants. The result is these tenants may choose not to rent your property.

Over the last few years, alternatives to traditional security deposits have surfaced in an attempt to remove that burden from renters. In Cincinnati, legislation called "Renter's Choice" passed in 2020 that requires landlords to offer something other than the traditional cash-up-front security.

Renter's Choice was the first law of its kind, and Atlanta followed suit several months later. Since then, many other states have proposed something like it. My experience tells me that alternatives to traditional security deposits will be a requirement in every state within a few years. Stay informed about these alternatives and get comfortable in dealing with them. While this trend continues to emerge, some confusion is likely to exist. Soon enough, however, they will become commonplace.

---

[24] LendingClub Corporation, "60% of Americans Now Living Paycheck to Paycheck, Down from 64% a Month Ago," news release, February 28, 2023, https://ir.lendingclub.com/news/news-details/2023/60-of-Americans-Now-Living-Paycheck-to-Paycheck-Down-from-64-a-Month-Ago/default.aspx#.

Installment agreements, surety bonds, rent guarantee, and credit authorization services have emerged as viable alternatives. Each of these has issues, but some have proven more effective than others.

INSTALLMENT AGREEMENTS

If someone cannot give you the entire security deposit up front and you think they will be a great tenant, you can remove the pressure by offering them an installment agreement.

Paying the security deposit in three, four, six, or more increments can be a much more amenable option for tenants. Suppose you are asking for $4,000 as a security deposit and the tenant does not have that amount of money prior to move-in. You could ask them to pay an extra $1,000 per month for four months, or $500 over eight months. You can set the term to be as long or as short as you want.

One thing to be careful with regarding installments is to use your best judgment when evaluating the tenant's ability to pay the extra monthly charges. Maybe you like a particular applicant and want to cut them a break, thinking it will be no problem for them to pay an extra $500 per month. There is a red flag, however, with almost any tenant who does not have sufficient savings to cover a security deposit: they might struggle to pay the extra monthly fee as well. Your flexibility, in this case, may result in the tenant getting behind on rent, which may cause you additional headaches down the road.

SURETY BONDS

Some companies provide a service where they will charge a tenant around 20% of the full security deposit. In return, the company agrees to pay for any damage caused by the tenant or for any amount in which they are in default of the lease.

You might think of this arrangement as an insurance policy where the tenant pays the premium. In reality, a surety bond allows the tenant to pay a small monthly fee rather than one large chunk of money up front. As the landlord, you are still protected against damage or nonpayment if the tenant causes any damage or has unpaid rent when they vacate.

Surety bonds have been around for a long time but have never been widely adopted. The legalese with anything this close to an insurance policy gets complicated, which leaves the renter and the landlord confused. This complexity makes it unlikely that the residential rental industry will settle on surety bonds as its chosen method for security deposit alternatives.

RENT GUARANTEE

Similar to a surety bond, a third party can act as a cosigner guaranteeing to pay for damages or nonpayment on the tenant's behalf. In my experience, rent guarantees are not ideal alternatives because they are difficult for a tenant to qualify for.

Rent guarantees can also be troublesome for you because they create an additional party you need to track down in the event of damage or nonpayment. Even when the third party is perfectly agreeable to signing the rent guarantee, they are much less willing to actually honor the agreement and pay for the tenant's damage or missing rent.

CREDIT AUTHORIZATION SERVICES

The winner among the currently available options appears to be something called a credit authorization service. The tenant applies with a company using a credit card and a bank account. That company then verifies the validity of the accounts. Once the company determines that the bank account is real and the credit card has room for additional charges, they agree to pay the landlord for any damages or unpaid rent or fees.

If any costly damage happens, you will file a claim with the credit authorization service. Once the claim is processed, you get your money in a relatively short time.

This is a good solution because you—the landlord—receive the peace of mind of knowing that a reputable company will pay you for whatever you are owed. It also benefits the tenant because the monthly fee is usually quite affordable, around $10 to $25 per month per $1,000 of credit offered.

Some companies require the first full year of fees to be paid up front. Although not ideal in the eyes of many tenants, paying $540 is preferable over paying a full security deposit ($45 per month for twelve months up front is still much more desirable than $4,000.) Tenants must remember, however, that this is a fee and they will not get their money back. In fact, it might be beneficial to eliminate any confusion by clearly stating that to your potential tenants if they elect to use this option.

The bottom line with credit authorization services is that they basically act as a credit card for renters. This is a newer product and the kinks still need to be worked out, as there is a fairly big variance in what some tenants pay per month compared to others.

None of these options—surety bonds, installation agreements, rental guarantee, or credit authorization services—are perfect. They are, however, a great starting point for renters and landlords to find creative ways to get around the overwhelming chunk of money that a traditional security deposit represents.

When any new process begins, there are advantages and disadvantages to consider. Understand what they are and you will have a foundation of knowledge to begin offering these services.

ADVANTAGES

Alternatives to security deposits have surfaced because of an unmet need. Almost eight out of every ten renters simply cannot pay all that cash up front. Using an alternative is a big advantage for the tenant because they can move into a new apartment more quickly. With a traditional security deposit, some people may need to save for many months before having enough money to sign a lease.

As the landlord, you get the advantage of a larger pool of potential applicants for your rental units. You are bringing in 78% of people who otherwise would not be able to rent your apartment. Going forward, landlords seeking to maximize profits must at least consider using alternative approaches to security deposits.

DISADVANTAGES

Renters should not look at security deposit alternatives as a way of getting away with unpaid damages. The lease still binds them to pay for anything that is broken or for unpaid fees. This is not a disadvantage, but more of a reminder that tenants should understand.

Landlords and tenants must deal with a modicum of added complexity when using alternatives to security deposits. At first, the terms and rights of these solutions can be confusing. In fact, we had to change the terms of our lease to accommodate the possibility of security deposit alternatives. If you use our sample lease in Appendix A, this added language is there for you to use or modify as needed.

The biggest disadvantage for a tenant is that all payments are nonrefundable. A traditional security deposit will be returned to them in full as long as there are no damages or unpaid rent. If the tenant opts for a surety bond or the use of a credit authorization service, they are paying a fee every month.

A FINAL WORD ON SECURITY DEPOSITS

You should pay careful attention to how you manage security deposits, as they can cause legal and financial headaches when they are mismanaged.

Consider the alternatives seriously, as the industry is definitely trending in that direction. More renters are going to want flexibility in how they get into an apartment. Keep an eye out for new companies coming up with bold solutions as well. Right now, security deposits are a painful point for a lot of tenants. Where painful points exist, innovation emerges to provide a game-changing solution.

You likely now have a deeper understanding of security deposits than 90% of other landlords in America. With this knowledge, you should be able to avoid the confusion and problems they can cause.

In the next chapter, you will acquire tips on how to handle maintenance requests and property inspections, which is another critical area for you to understand when attempting to maximize profits as a landlord.

CHAPTER 9

MAINTENANCE REQUESTS, PROPERTY INSPECTIONS, AND RENTAL LICENSE

L andlords have a duty (called an implied warranty of habitability) to keep their rental property in good, habitable, and safe working order. Although the specific requirements will differ slightly by state, you have a general responsibility to make sure all the systems are operating as intended and the premise is safe, sanitary, and reasonably comfortable.[25] It is important that you know the state and local rules to ensure full compliance at all times.

Maintenance services have two primary purposes. Making sure your property meets all the state and local requirements as mentioned above. But also, meeting your tenant's maintenance needs will make them happier, and happy tenants stay longer. According to a recent survey of our tenants, the lack of reply to maintenance requests is the number one reason they leave their apartments. So

---

[25] Erin Eberlin, "Do You Have What It Takes to Be a Landlord?" LiveAbout, last modified November 20, 2019, https://www.liveabout.com/what-is-a-landlord-duties-and-responsibilities-2125057.

simply responding to maintenance requests will contribute to your tenants staying longer. And as we should know at this point, profit maximization is a result of having as little vacancy as possible.

Safe, sanitary, and reasonably comfortable can be open to interpretation and sometimes might be a bit of a gray area. At a minimum, landlords are required to:

- Provide hot and cold running water without leaks
- Ensure all windows open, close, and lock correctly
- Ensure all doorways open and close properly and all locks are in working order
- Have GFI (ground fault interrupter) outlets near any running water
- Ensure all steps have secure and safe handrails without any tripping hazards
- Ensure all smoke and CO detectors are functioning properly and in compliance with state and local regulations
- Ensure common areas are well-lit, free from clutter, and safe (this also means ensuring the front door of a multiunit dwelling has some sort of security measure in place to prevent intruders)
- Resolve all routine maintenance issues in a reasonable time frame
- Respond quickly to all requests for emergency repairs that are life safety issues such as gas, electricity, plumbing, heating, ventilation, air conditioning, and appliances

This is only a quick list of big issues to keep in mind as a responsible landlord.

RESPONDING TO
MAINTENANCE REQUESTS

Although the requirements to keep an apartment safe for your tenants may seem extensive, do not let it overwhelm you. A big key to managing this is not to jump at every request for repairs. If the tenant has no heat in their apartment, you need to respond immediately. However, if the tenant has a kitchen cabinet that has come off the hinges, you do not need to call a contractor to respond within twenty-four hours. The essential items listed in the bullet points above should be addressed quickly, but almost everything else can wait a few days until your schedule allows you the time to respond.

It is crucial to document and follow up on every repair request. When you receive a notice from a tenant requesting a repair, send an email or text acknowledging that you have received the request and with your plan to address the issue(s).

Once you know who will be making the repairs and when, notify the tenant so they can be home to let the repair person in or allow them entry without being present. Once the repair is complete, send the tenant an email or text letting them know the job is done and ask if they have any further questions or concerns. Be sure to save all emails, texts, or letters after each maintenance request as proof of your diligence in the event that any repair or maintenance request results in a legal dispute or court case.

Types of Rental Property Maintenance Expenses

There are several different types of maintenance you will be required to perform on your rental properties. Now, the urgency may be different for the different types of maintenance, but expect all four of these types of maintenance at your rental property:

- **Routine Maintenance**–Most rental properties have various forms of routine maintenance that could occur at any time. These include heating and air-conditioning upkeep, malfunctioning appliances, and leaking toilets among other items. Snow removal, cutting the grass, and other landscaping activities are outdoor jobs considered routine maintenance.
- **Emergency Maintenance**–Repair work like burst pipes, backed-up toilets, and no heat must be addressed immediately because they could affect the tenant's safety.
- **Preventative Maintenance**–Consider maintenance service contracts for such services as HVAC, appliances, and pest control to perform regular inspections and repairs as needed. These services will reduce costs by minimizing repair work for routine and emergency maintenance issues.
- **Seasonal Maintenance**–This type of work will vary depending on the location and type of property you own. Examples include tree pruning, fall leaf removal, or gutter cleaning.

ESTIMATE YOUR MONTHLY MAINTENANCE BUDGET

There are a number of ways to estimate repairs on your rental property. Some are better than others, but throughout my career and seeing thousands of budgets, I almost always see owners underestimating the cost of repairs and maintenance.

The industry standard or rule of thumb is to allocate 1% of your total property value for repairs and maintenance costs per year. For example, if your property is worth $300,000, you should expect to pay about $3,000 per year to keep the property in good and safe living condition. Divide this annual figure by twelve months and you can budget about $250 per month to be set aside as for repair and maintenance.

Another rule of thumb is to allocate 10% of the monthly rent. If the above property rented for $3,000 per month you would budget $300 per month for repairs or $3,600 per year.

As mentioned above, you may want to budget even higher than these estimates to be sure your budget has enough to keep your property in reasonable working order. Properties that will need a higher budget might include those that are in high-crime neighborhoods, older properties, homes with a history of extensive repairs work, or properties with problems you already know about.

Also, keep in mind this budget amount is for normal maintenance as described above. You may also want to have a long-term reserve account for large repairs such as new roofs, large-scale improvements, new heaters, or other large expensive items that may not happen for years (see Chapter 14). These reserves can be as little as $25 to $50 per month, but that accumulates over time to offset the potentially large cost of expensive projects. You may want to set up a separate bank account to hold these reserve funds so they are separate from your normal operating funds.

PERFORM ROUTINE INSPECTIONS

Another way to prevent repairs and maintenance from piling up is to conduct routine inspections. Go into your apartments (giving your tenants ample notice, which is usually twenty-four hours) every three to six months and inspect the property to make sure all major systems are in working order and no damage has been done.

During these inspections, you should have a complete checklist, which should include the following (at a bare minimum):

- Furnace filters
- Smoke and CO detectors (check or replace batteries)
- Fire extinguishers
- Signs of bugs/pests
- Water leaks (sink, toilet, faucets, and roof)
- Water damage (walls, ceiling, and floors)
- Running toilets
- Windows and doors are operating correctly
- Appliances are working properly
- Overall cleanliness and condition of the unit

You can also ask the tenant if anything is not working properly and record that as part of your property inspection. You will find the vast majority of necessary repairs and maintenance items simply by doing your routine property inspections.

If you are unable to perform these inspections, you can hire a third-party vendor to do it and provide you with a report. Have the person performing the inspection complete your property checklist and instruct them to take pictures or videos as they go through each apartment. This will give you a detailed record of the condition of the property every few months.

REQUESTS FOR ALTERATIONS AND IMPROVEMENTS

Some tenants want to make alterations to the unit such as painting walls a different color, adding a storm door, replacing appliances or making other enhancements because they plan to live there for an extended period.

You should handle each request as a unique circumstance. Have them send a letter or fill out a form that states exactly what they plan to do and decide whether to grant their request. Most people simply want to paint the bedroom a different color or make other small changes. Minor alterations like these should be granted without much time or effort on your part.

Major alterations, however, should be carefully considered. For example, if the tenant wants to knock down a wall from the kitchen to the living space, that is likely something you want to decline.

SITUATIONS TO AVOID

Some landlords like to add to their lease that the tenant will pay the first $50 to $200 for each repair. The hope is this will reduce the number of maintenance requests. We do not recommend this policy for a couple of reasons.

First, most repair items are legally your responsibility as the landlord. If a tenant wants you to repair a nonworking stove, they are well within their legal rights to have you fix it in a timely manner. Second, our experience with this policy will do the opposite—the tenant will simply not call in maintenance requests and problems will not get fixed. Third, the fees can add up and become difficult to track. For example, if you go to fix one item and find several other items that need to be repaired, do you charge this fee one time, or three or four times for each item? Finally, judges also will likely not grant your fee for repairs if there was ever a dispute about these charges in court.

Another situation to avoid is having tenants do repairs for you. It is fine to ask them to cut the grass if you are renting a single-family home. You can also ask them to perform other small jobs like patching paint, fixing a loose doorknob, and taking the trash street side. If tenants agree to perform any of these minor tasks, you can pay them directly or give them a credit on their rent to reward them for their due diligence.

THIRD-PARTY REPAIR SERVICES

For any repair or maintenance work that extends beyond those extremely minor jobs, you have a couple of choices:

1. Do the work yourself if you are especially handy and have enough time to do it,
2. Or hire a third-party vendor who comes with solid reviews and at a reasonable price.

If you cannot do the work yourself, you should have a list of third-party vendors in your contact list so you can call someone to fix problems as soon as they arise. In other words, ensure you have a good plumber, electrician, etc. on standby whenever you need them.

UNMET REPAIR NEEDS

Tenants are well within their legal rights to take action if the premises are unfit to live in and you do not respond in a timely manner to their request for repairs. One such action is that your tenant has the right to place their rent in escrow.

Similarly to how landlords handle security deposits, tenants must place their rent money in an escrow account. The account should be labeled "Rent Escrow." The tenant may even have to provide a bank statement proving the money is in escrow while the landlord fixes the unacceptable problem(s).

Ultimately, your tenant could bring in an inspector to verify the apartment as unfit, file a lawsuit, and move out. Whether or not they owe you any rent at that point would be up to the court to decide. Obviously, this is a situation you want to avoid. Not only is it not going to maximize your profits (because you will probably lose such a court case), but it is also not the right way to handle the responsibilities of being a professional landlord.

One of the things I mentioned earlier in the book was how landlords perform a necessary societal function by giving people a place to live and potentially raise their families. The personal sense of reward you get from fulfilling that role only exists if you provide people with a safe, clean, and comfortable environment.

RENTAL LICENSE TO RENT YOUR APARTMENT

Most (not all) cities and townships require landlords to acquire a rental license to rent an apartment. Check with your local township to ensure you are properly licensed to act as a landlord.

Additionally, the local authorities may need to inspect your property, and they are mostly looking for life safety issues. They will test and check fire extinguishers, handrails, sidewalks and steps, doors and locks, and make sure windows and latches are in working order. They will also examine smoke detectors and carbon monoxide detectors, and ensure that the bathrooms and kitchen have working ground fault interrupters (GFI) on the outlets near sinks, tubs, and showers.

In some areas, you may need to hire a lead paint expert to inspect the apartment and provide a certificate that states the absence of lead paint in the apartment. Some areas may also require a plumber to inspect the heater and water heater and ensure they are in good, working order.

These extra required documents might sound like a lot, but it only takes a few phone calls to get the right people to come out to your apartment and approve it for occupancy. You could call these things necessary evils, but in reality, they protect you from catastrophe. For example, if the heater at your rental property is old and begins to leak carbon monoxide, serious complications can occur. These township inspections are another way to protect yourself as a landlord to be sure your property is in safe, working order.

A FINAL WORD ON REPAIR AND MAINTENANCE REQUESTS

The best way to handle repair and maintenance requests is to abide by the advice that pertains to the other items in this book: have a clearly defined system in place and stick with it. Rely on your lease in times of doubt and you should be able to avoid most problems getting out of control.

Now that you have a foundation of knowledge to get your apartments occupied, collect rent, and maintain the property, it is time to go through the best ways to conduct a tenant move-in and move-out in the next chapter.

CHAPTER 10

TENANT MOVE-IN AND MOVE-OUT

There are usually a lot of moving parts that need to be coordinated on move-in day for both the tenant and landlord. In addition to movers showing up on time, utilities must be switched over to the new tenant, paperwork must be signed, and money must be collected.

As the landlord, you need to prepare as much as possible to avoid some of the stress on move-in day. Let this chapter serve as your reference guide to your move-in and move-out procedures.

TENANT MOVE-IN

To start, I recommend sending the tenant a welcome letter a week or two prior to move-in by both email and regular mail. I have included a sample welcome letter in Appendix D. This document should contain vital information like confirming the move-in date, what money is due prior to move-in day, and how to pay. In addition, the welcome letter should include key items such as a reminder to have utilities turned on in their name, what day the trash is collected, where the mail is picked up, and how maintenance requests should be handled.

The welcome letter is a nice way to introduce your tenant to you and their new apartment and shows you as a professional landlord. This also gives you a week or two prior to move-in to make sure your files are in order, all the paperwork is complete and signed, and any remaining monies have been paid. From there, move-in day should go much smoother.

COMPLETE ALL PAPERWORK

Renting an apartment does not involve the same amount of paperwork as buying a home, but there are quite a few different documents that need to be signed. In our standard lease, the tenants must initial in four separate spots and sign in eight to ten different spots on the lease and the various addendums.

Some local townships or cities may have additional documents that must be signed. For example, in Philadelphia, landlords must provide tenants with a pamphlet called "Partners for Good Housing" that instructs them on how to be a good tenant. Failure to provide this document to a tenant will block your ability to evict them later, if needed. We require our tenants to sign this document, giving us proof we provided the tenant a copy.

CONDUCT A PRE-INSPECTION A FEW DAYS AHEAD

A couple of days before the tenant is scheduled to move in, conduct a thorough pre-inspection. This inspection should take less than an hour to make sure the cleaners did their job and any repair work was done satisfactorily.

If you do not walk through the apartment ahead of time, you are trusting your team did everything as per your instructions. As an experienced landlord, I have found it is better to "trust but verify" they have done their work to your satisfaction. Without a pre-inspection you might get a call from the tenant complaining that the carpets are dirty or the leaky faucet was not fixed. And then you are off to a bad start. Plan on doing an inspection a week or so prior to move-in day. That way, if something was left undone, you still have time to address the problem before the tenant sees it.

As part of the pre-inspection, I would also take photos or a video to document the condition of the unit prior to move-in. Hopefully, you never have a dispute with your tenant that ends up in court, but these pictures will show a judge what the apartment looked like before the tenant moved in. This could be key to showing that the tenant is responsible for any damages.

COLLECT MONEY

Another thing that should be taken care of before move-in day is to collect any remaining money the tenant may owe. It becomes a big problem when the tenant shows up on moving day owing $2,500 and says, "I apologize. I only have $2,000 today, but I can get the other $500 by next week."

This situation is why you must collect the tenant's money prior to move-in day. You do not want any last-minute excuses. If they show up on move-in day with movers and kids waiting to claim their new bedrooms, it will be hard to tell them they cannot have the keys without all the money being paid up front.

ESTABLISH COMMUNICATION

Clarify how you will communicate with the tenant after move-in. In some situations, sending letters through the mail may be necessary for legal purposes, but it is inconvenient and slow. Email is preferable, but also get a phone number to use text messaging. You can then send a quick text when you need your tenants to let a repair worker into the apartment or to alert them of an issue.

TENANT MOVE-OUT

If you select good renters, odds are they will stay in your apartment for several years without too many problems during their stay. But at some point their lease term will come to an end and one of three things can happen:

1. The tenant could choose to sign a new one- or two-year lease with a rent increase as discussed in Chapter 3.
2. Both parties could agree to a month-to-month lease agreement.
3. You or the tenant can terminate the lease with sixty or ninety days written notice.

In our sample lease in Appendix A, you will see our lease automatically converts to a month-to-month lease at the end of the term if the tenant does not agree to a new lease. When this happens, the rent goes up by 10% automatically. Therefore, it benefits the tenants to sign a new lease if they plan on staying in the apartment for more than a few months.

GET LEASE TERMINATION IN WRITING

As we have talked about before, be sure to get a termination notice in writing and do not accept a verbal agreement to terminate the lease. Some landlords like to send an email that says, "Your lease is scheduled to terminate on June 30." If the tenant does not respond, this leaves the door open to miscommunication. Unless you get a confirmation to your email, the lease is not terminated and will continue on a month-to-month basis. To avoid potential problems associated with email, I recommend you get any notice to terminate in writing.

The best way to handle lease termination is to provide the tenant with a move-out letter and ask them to return it with their signature by a certain date. In the letter, include a reference to the section of the lease that provides the road map for getting their security deposit back (see Chapter 8).

MOVE-OUT INSPECTIONS

After the tenant moves out, perform a thorough inspection within the first week after the lease ends. Do not allow the tenant to be present for this inspection because it can create an awkward situation. If you inspect the apartment together and they see that you are going to charge them for cleaning the carpet or fixing a broken sink, you do not want to get into an argument. Conduct your inspections alone or through a third party, but never have the tenant walk through with you or your representative.

While conducting your move-out inspection, make sure that the apartment was cleaned to a satisfactory level and look for any damage that is beyond normal wear and tear. You can charge for any repairs or extra cleaning that is above normal wear and tear against their security deposit as discussed in Chapter 8.

The security deposit issue can be confusing for most landlords, and some of the information is worth repeating here. At the end of a tenant's lease, you, the landlord, have the right to keep a portion of the security deposit for any damage, unpaid rent, or late fees. If the tenant owes you $175 in late fees, it comes off the security deposit. If they owe you two months of unpaid rent, that comes off the security deposit as well. If they caused $700 worth of damage and the apartment needs extra cleaning, those items also come off the security deposit.

A FINAL WORD ON TENANT MOVE-IN AND MOVE-OUT

In this chapter we discussed the necessary steps for a smooth tenant move-in and move-out process. Landlords should send a welcome letter with essential information and ensure all paperwork is completed before move-in day. They should also conduct a pre-inspection to verify the unit's condition and collect outstanding payments from the tenant. Establishing a communication method is crucial for effective management. When tenants move out, lease termination should be in writing, and a move-out inspection should be conducted without the tenant present to assess any damages or necessary deductions from the security deposit.

In the next chapter, we will discuss everything you need to know about insurance. As a landlord, this is crucial to protecting your business and personal assets. Learn about the various options for different policies and enjoy the peace of mind of knowing that you are covered.

CHAPTER 11

PROTECTING YOURSELF WITH INSURANCE

Insurance is one of those critical areas where you want some knowledge to protect yourself and your investment properties against a potentially large financial loss. We know that real estate investors and landlords are sued more than any other business. So it makes sense to prepare yourself against some of these risks. And it starts with a trustworthy and reputable insurance advisor as part of your team and some basic knowledge on your part. The following chapter will provide you with a basic understanding of this topic.

First, a story about what can happen if you are not properly insured.

A LANDLORD HORROR STORY

Many years ago, my company was hired to manage a rental home that had an outdoor deck on the third floor. One of the tenants had been drinking and went out to the deck, laid down on a lounge chair, lit a cigarette, and fell asleep—and the deck and roof caught on fire.

The good news was that everyone (including the tenant who fell asleep) escaped unharmed. The bad news was that the third floor and roof were just about destroyed, and the entire house needed to be repainted due to water damage. Additionally, the landlord was also unable to rent the property for several months while repairs were being made, causing even more lost income.

You might be thinking that all the landlord had to do was file a claim with their insurance company, pay the deductible, and recoup most of their losses. Unfortunately, that was not the case.

A few days after the accident, the owner of the building told me that they never informed the insurance company they were not living in the building. Most homeowner's insurance policies require the homeowner to live in the property or the policy is voidable. This meant that the landlord could not claim the damage. The loss was financially devastating at over $30,000.

As a landlord, you need to let your insurer know if you are not occupying the property. This is the difference between homeowner's insurance and landlord's insurance, which costs $200 to $300 extra per year. Why? Renters are temporary occupants and will generally not treat the property as well as a homeowner would. Therefore, the insurer is likely to pay more in claims on a rental property than for a home where the owner actually lives.

The moral of the story is to not leave yourself or your property vulnerable, as the inordinately high risk is simply not worth the slight savings of the cheaper policy.

ACTUAL CASH VALUE VERSUS
REPLACEMENT COST VALUE INSURANCE

Most insurance providers offer replacement value or cash value property insurance where any property damage will be covered after a loss, subject to certain limitations. While both types of coverage help with the costs of rebuilding or repairing your property, actual cash value policies are based on the item's "depreciated value," while replacement cost coverage covers in today's dollars.

Actual Cash Value (AVC)—An AVC policy will *reimburse* you for the replacement cost of the damaged property less the depreciation over the years and the policy deductible. For example, if you own a twenty-year-old building that is destroyed, the insurance company may say that 50% of the property's value is gone. In that case, they would pay 50% of the property's original value and you would need to pay the difference if you choose to rebuild. So the amount you would receive from your insurer after a covered claim may not be equal to the cost of replacing or rebuilding your property at today's prices.

Replacement Cost Value (RCV)—An RCV policy will *replace* whatever gets damaged in today's dollars. If you purchased a property for $200,000 twenty years ago and it burns down, the insurer will pay to rebuild the property less any deductible or other fees. Individual policies can have a great deal of variance, so check with your insurance advisor for the exact parameters of your policy.

Regardless of what type of coverage you have, you will pay a deductible before your insurance coverage kicks in. Both types of coverage are subject to limits, which is the maximum amount your policy will pay toward a covered loss. Review your policy with your insurance advisors to be sure you understand which type of coverage your policy provides as well as the amount of your deductible and coverage limits.

So which type of policy is right for you?

The answer depends on what you hope to accomplish with your rental properties. Most investors want to—at least—consider an RCV policy to protect against inflation. It is going to cost a little more, but if you want to sleep well at night and not worry about one of your tenants accidently doing something extremely damaging, the extra money is worth it.

If your property has a mortgage on it, the bank will require an RCV policy. The lender will not want to be in a situation where their loan might not get repaid if the building is irreparable.

BASIC (DP1), BROAD (DP2), AND SPECIAL (DP3) INSURANCE FORMS

If you choose RCV insurance, you have three options—Basic, Broad, or Special forms, which are also referred to as DP1, DP2, and DP3 in the insurance world. The numbers go from low to high to reflect the scale of coverage.

Basic (DP1) insurance will cover your property against specifically listed incidents. Because it covers the least, a DP1 policy is often the cheapest, but also the riskiest. Most often, it will not cover theft/robbery, fallen trees, or frozen pipes.[26] These are fairly common occurrences and that fact steers many investors away

---

[26] Hippo, "What Is a DP1 Home Insurance Policy?," accessed May 24, 2023, https://www.hippo.com/learn-center/dp1-home-insurance/.

from basic insurance, particularly in the Northeast where frozen pipes are known to become financially debilitating if not listed on your policy.

Broad (DP2) insurance offers more extensive coverage than DP1. Although it is not used often, it can be considered a midrange policy. It will cover damage from frozen pipes, but it is still limited in that it will cover only specifically listed incidents.[27]

Special (DP3) insurance is a comprehensive policy that most investors choose because it covers everything except for clearly noted exclusions. The most notable of these are earthquakes and floods, but you should still check with your insurance advisor.[28]

Water Damage and Lost Rent Insurance Rider

If you live in a flood zone, insurance companies and lenders will require an addendum that covers water damage from floods. There are ranges of flood zones, of which you will need to check with your provider for more specific information.

You can purchase additional insurance to cover water damage no matter where you live, but the cost of such protection can be quite expensive. Nonetheless, it does not hurt to ask your insurance advisors about what the specific additional premium would be for your particular property.

You can also choose to add a lost rent rider to most landlord policies. This rider can reimburse you for lost rent in the event your

---

[27] Kin, "DP2 Policy," accessed May 24, 2023, https://www.kin.com/glossary/dp2-policy/.

[28] Advanced Insurance Services, "DP 1 Policy VS DP 3 Policy," accessed May 24, 2023, https://www.aisagency.com/dp1-vs-dp3.html.

property becomes uninhabitable for a period of time. The amount usually ranges from six to twelve months, depending on the policy you chose.

LANDLORD'S PERSONAL BELONGINGS

Although a DP3 policy will cover some of the landlord's personal belongings, it may not cover everything. Therefore, if you have a lawn mower, tools, and other high-cost supplies kept in a shed or garage, consult your insurance advisor to confirm that these items will be covered.

RENTER'S INSURANCE

Renter insurance is insurance that covers the tenants' personal belongings and liability. Requiring tenants to have renter insurance has become a common practice among landlords, and for good reason. Renter's insurance generally only costs the tenant about $150 to $300 per year with a deductible of $250 to $500 per occurrence.

Included in our sample lease in Appendix A, section 19 titled Tenant's Personal Property and Insurance is where the tenant is required to have renter's insurance and to initial this section of the lease to show the importance.

Renter insurance can provide several benefits for landlords.

Firstly, renter insurance can provide protection for the tenants' personal belongings. In the event of theft, damage or loss, tenants will be able to make a claim on their insurance policy to recover their losses, rather than looking to the landlord for compensation. This can help to reduce the risk of disputes between landlords and tenants and can also reduce the overall cost of repairs and replacements for the landlord.

Secondly, renter insurance can provide protection for the landlord in the event of a liability claim. For example, if a tenant's guest is injured while visiting the rental property, the tenant's renter insurance policy may provide coverage for any legal costs and damages that may be awarded. This can help to protect the landlord from financial liability and can also reduce the risk of costly lawsuits.

Thirdly, requiring tenants to have renter insurance can help to reduce the risk of damage to rental properties. Tenants with renter insurance are often more diligent about taking care of their personal belongings and the rental property itself, as they have a financial interest in protecting their assets. This can result in less damages and repairs required by the landlord, reducing your overall costs and increasing their profits.

One thing you may run into is, even if your lease requires renter's insurance, many tenants will not actually get it or will allow it to lapse. But as long as your lease requires renter's insurance, the tenant will not be able to come after the landlord for any damage to the tenants' belongings.

LIABILITY COVERAGE

Property damage will cover any damage to your property but does not protect you against someone getting injured on your property. As a landlord, it is essential to have both property insurance and liability coverage.

Personal injury claims are usually far more costly than those related to property damage. If someone gets burned, falls down the stairs, or suffers another life-affecting injury, they may require lifelong medical attention, which can be quite financially costly.

If a twenty-year-old individual gets injured on your property to the point where they can no longer work, they need to recoup a salary for the rest of their life. If you do not have liability coverage, this could put you on the hook for $75,000 (or whatever their annual salary was) every year for the next thirty years. That is not a situation in which you want to be.

A good insurance policy with liability coverage protects you from legal and medical costs incurred from an injury on your property. This could be a tenant, a guest, or anyone else. If anyone gets hurt on your property, you could be liable for the healthcare bills. The determining factor usually hinges on whether the injured party can prove that you were negligent in not performing needed maintenance or repair work.

The key takeaway is that although liability coverage is not considered mandatory by state law, we strongly advise all landlords to protect their financial assets with liability coverage.

At Del Val, we *require* our landlords to carry $500,000 in liability insurance. But we actually *recommend* a million or more as the price difference of $500,000 to $1 million in liability is relatively small.

DAMAGE CAUSED BY TENANTS

A potential gray area is when your tenant causes damage to your property. Most often, it is the result of an accident. For example, your tenant might have a dog or cat that runs out of an open door. Perhaps the tenant left the stove on to chase after them and something catastrophic happened. That incident is likely claimable because it is classified as an accident.

If, however, a tenant intentionally causes damage in the form of vandalism, the insurance provider will likely not cover it. And if you are a landlord long enough you may have a tenant do intentional damage on the way out.

Perhaps you have to evict someone because they are not paying their rent, violating your rules, or any number of other reasons. They might get angry, seek retribution, and decide to pour cement down the tub drain or break the pipes. Insurance is only intended to protect you against accidental damage or unforeseen events. When a tenant causes damage on purpose, it may not be claimable. Your recourse in these cases is to take the tenant to court. And even if you have proof with pictures, winning in court is not a certainty.

CARRY AN UMBRELLA PLAN FOR EXTRA COVERAGE

An Excess Liability Coverage (umbrella) policy can provide extra liability coverage in all insurable areas including investment properties, homes, autos, and more. This is not to be confused with your standard landlord's insurance; it is a secondary policy for added protection. For example, suppose you got into a car accident that caused $11,000 in damages, but had only $10,000 worth of coverage on your auto policy. If you had an umbrella policy, it would kick in to cover the remaining cost.

Umbrella policies are usually quite inexpensive. They are a wise choice, especially for investors and homeowners who have a lot of financial assets to protect. Some nuances exist, however, which makes umbrella coverage another area you should address with your insurance advisor. Ask questions and know exactly what you are paying for and how it helps you.

A FINAL WORD ON INSURANCE

The bottom line regarding insurance is to do your homework and make sure you have an exceptional insurance advisor. The cost of the premiums should be less of a consideration than the type and amount of insurance you have.

As a landlord, insurance is *not* the area to cut corners. In fact, maximizing profits often means making smart decisions and being proactive, rather than finding areas to trim a few dollars.

Besides insurance and conducting regular walk-arounds to inspect properties, you can take other precautions and actions to avoid risk, which will be covered in the next chapter.

CHAPTER 12

HOW TO AVOID RISK AS A LANDLORD

I n the last chapter, we discussed how property and liability insurance can protect you if something happens to your property or someone is injured on the premises. We also mentioned how an umbrella policy can provide additional protection.

Insurance is the landlord's first line of defense against financial risk. However, there are a number of other preventative actions and measures you can take to reduce your risk as a property owner. Implementing these measures as a complement to your insurance coverage will provide protection for your rental property investments.

PROPERTY INSPECTIONS:
WHAT YOU DON'T KNOW *CAN* HURT YOU

To avoid or minimize liability claims, it is a best practice to walk around your properties (common areas and individual apartments) several times per year, looking for problems and recording the conditions in a written report or, even better, with photos. During these property inspections, check for the following:

- Cracks or uneven sections of a sidewalk that could pose a tripping hazard
- Poor lighting, particularly in walkways, driveways, and hallways
- Unsecured railings to stairways
- Toys, barbecue grills, and other debris left carelessly in common areas that could cause people to stumble and fall
- Any lingering repair issues
- The GFI outlets are in working order
- Snow and ice removal
- Dead batteries or nonworking smoke and carbon monoxide detectors
- Aggressive dogs (see Chapter 6)
- Any signs of water leaks from the roof or internal plumbing

These property inspections generally take less than an hour and can eliminate many liability issues by simply walking around your own property and taking corrective action to repair any issues.

ENCOURAGE TENANTS TO REPORT REPAIR ISSUES QUICKLY

One small thing you can do to save yourself a lot of headaches as a landlord is repeatedly encourage your tenants to report any damages or potential problems.

Many tenants tend to ignore things that do not directly affect them. For example, a tenant on the third floor of a multiunit dwelling might have a drip coming from a pipe in the kitchen. They may not report it because it does not affect them. A few months later, the tenant on the second floor may discover a section of their drywall getting damp. One day, the drywall completely crumbles and falls. What would have been $150 to fix a leaky pipe now becomes a $2,000 repair of the drywall, testing for mold, and fixing the leaky pipe.

That situation could have been avoided if the tenant had reported the problem right away. By encouraging tenants to do this, you also build a good rapport with them as they know you are a good landlord who will do what it takes to ensure a safe and comfortable living space for them.

AVOID FAIR HOUSING VIOLATIONS

We discussed this briefly in Chapter 3, and it is essential that you know the Fair Housing rules and put procedures in place to avoid violations.

Federal and state Fair Housing laws prevent actions that might be considered discriminatory practices when accepting or declining a prospective tenant. The federal Fair Housing Act prohibits discrimination based on race or color, national origin, sex, religion, familial status, and disability. Your state may also have additional protected classes.

When you are making a decision to accept or decline a potential tenant, it is important that you treat all applicants the same. As discussed earlier, we have a point system that we use to be sure we are treating all applicants the same.

A landlord should not:

- Tell someone a property is not available when it is actually available for rent
- Exclude a group of people in your advertising, i.e., "only Section 8" or "adults only"
- Create different terms or standards for certain tenants
- Refuse to accept a tenant for one of the above protected classes

Be aware of the Fair Housing laws and review all ads and communications with prospective tenants to be sure you are not violating any of the above.

Source of Income

There is currently a movement by the Department of Housing and Urban Development (HUD) and other federal agencies to make "source of income" a protected class. This would include any tenant that is part of the Section 8 program or similar programs. If implemented, it would not allow landlords to decline an applicant due to their source of income. I expect in the next few years that this proposal will become federal law.

WORKERS' COMPENSATION INSURANCE

Another important risk-reducing behavior is to require anyone who works on your property, including repairmen and contractors, to show you a certificate that proves they have adequate liability coverage and workers' compensation insurance.

The penalties for a landlord hiring a contractor without workers' compensation insurance can be serious enough to include criminal charges. If a contractor gets injured on your property, you might need to pay their medical bills as well as any legal costs to defend yourself in court.

ENVIRONMENTAL HEALTH HAZARDS

All landlords have a legal obligation to protect tenants from environmental hazards like asbestos, carbon monoxide, radon, lead paint, and bedbugs. To comply with federal and state laws, it is important to mitigate these risks by taking action to prevent harm to your tenants.

ASBESTOS

In older buildings, asbestos can be a serious issue. A property built before 1980 may have contained some form of the deadly fibers in the insulation of pipes, floors, drywall, roofs, or siding.

A lung cancer known as mesothelioma has been linked to asbestos exposure. The best way to determine whether it exists on your property is to test for it. A lot of information is available on the Internet about how to test for asbestos yourself. However, I recommend you hire an outside expert to conduct the testing.

Professional testing companies will come in, collect samples, and test for asbestos. This service is not exorbitantly expensive. Of course, if your property turns out to have the substance, you then need to have it removed, repaired, and/or encapsulated. We recommend hiring experts to perform the removal process as well.

CARBON MONOXIDE

Another deadly chemical that can cause extreme sickness and even death is carbon monoxide. It can seep into the air of a property, usually due to a malfunctioning heater. Depending on the type, brand, and quality of your heater, they usually last around ten to fifteen years. Once they start to malfunction, carbon monoxide could leak into the property.

Most local laws now require working carbon monoxide and smoke detectors to be installed on all floors including the basement. Fortunately, a single device will test for both today. They usually cost around $40 to $60 and come with ten-year batteries that are encapsulated into the device and cannot be removed.

We recommend you have your heater tested by a heater/plumber certified in these types of inspections. If the system does not pass due to carbon monoxide, seek a professional to advise you if it is repairable or must be replaced.

RADON

When you buy a property, you usually have the right to test for dangerously high levels of radon before finalizing the sale.

Radon is a naturally occurring radioactive gas that can cause lung cancer. The gas is inert, colorless, and odorless. Trace amounts occur naturally in the atmosphere, but radon becomes a health risk when it gets trapped in a building after entering through cracks and other holes in the foundation.[29]

---

[29] United States Environmental Protection Agency, "What Is Radon Gas? Is It Dangerous?," last modified October 24, 2022, https://www.epa.gov/radiation/what-radon-gas-it-dangerous.

Similar to asbestos, you can test for radon yourself by purchasing a testing kit for about $60. If remediation is needed, you should outsource the job to an experienced professional as it usually involves sealing up cracks and holes in the foundation.

MOLD

Asbestos, carbon monoxide, and radon gas have urgency associated with their terms. They sound dangerous and people recognize them as such. In comparison, mold sounds relatively harmless, but it is not.

You must take mold seriously as it poses a serious health threat. When allowed to spread to an uncontrollable level, it can destroy an entire property.

Mold is always the result of moisture collecting in a confined space. Common occurrences of mold come from a hole in the roof, a leaky toilet, or something going wrong with a tub, shower, refrigerator, or sink.

If a tenant complains that they smell mold, you should hire someone to test for it immediately. If they discover mold, they can remove and remediate the mold. You also need to find and repair the original leak or water penetration to ensure the mold does not return.

LEAD PAINT

In 1978, lead-based paint, which has been known to cause severe damage to vital organs, was outlawed. Therefore, any house built prior to that date likely has it. Local laws may differ, but in Philadelphia property owners who rent to tenants must conduct a test for the presence of lead paint.

There are two forms of lead paint tests. You can get a "lead-free" or "lead-safe" certification. A lead-free certificate is good for the life of the property. It usually costs a few hundred dollars more than the lead-safe test, which must be done every four years.

Unlike some of the other issues mentioned in this chapter, you cannot conduct your own lead paint test. You must hire a certified lead paint professional. We also recommend you use a lead paint disclosure form (see our sample lease) to ensure you are in compliance with federal law. This disclosure must be kept for three years but does not need to be updated if the tenant renews the lease for additional years.

BEDBUGS

Ten years ago, bedbugs were a huge problem. Since then, property owners have become more proactive in eliminating the issue and we see less bedbugs now than in previous years.

Check your local laws to be certain about bedbugs. In Philadelphia, the landlord must pay for all remediation related to bedbugs for up to one year from the tenant's move-in date. This is an exception to the pests' clause in our sample lease that declares the tenant's responsibility for any problems after thirty days.

Professionals can come into your property to do the proper testing and extermination, but the cost can be significant. It can be a tough pill to swallow when you need to pay for remediation of bedbugs that surfaced ninety days after a tenant moved in, but you have to chalk it up as another cost of doing business.

CRIMINAL ACTIVITY

Landlords are not required to act as security guards for their properties. However, it is in your best interest to take all precautions possible to prevent any criminal activity from occurring in or around your building. Several measures have already been discussed that you can use to accomplish this. These include the following:

- Proper lighting around the building's exterior and in all common areas
- Deadbolt locks on doors
- Properly functioning window locks
- Security systems
- Perform regular property inspections
- Educate tenants about potential crime in the neighborhood
- Handle complaints from tenants about dangerous situations
- Run criminal background checks as part of your application process

Even if you attend to all those issues with the utmost attention to detail, crime can still find its way into a property. Keep your eyes open and make sure you report any suspicious activity to the local police. You can also make your neighbors an ally. Form a friendly rapport with them, and they will inform you if they see a lot of nighttime visitors coming in and out of your building.

Our lease includes a drug-free addendum, which states that any drug activity is a material breach of the lease and could result in termination of the lease and eviction. Invoke that clause anytime you feel it is necessary.

A FINAL WORD ON AVOIDING RISK

There is no way to avoid all risk as a landlord. Unforeseen circumstances are going to pop up occasionally. You can, however, follow the advice in this chapter to minimize the likelihood of any troublesome situations arising. With due diligence and a good insurance policy as stated in the previous chapter, you will maximize profits with peace of mind.

In the next chapter, you will learn about common legal issues and how to deal with them. Similar to having a good insurance advisor, if you have a good lawyer, this will also add to your protections.

CHAPTER 13

COMMON LANDLORD LEGAL ISSUES AND HOW TO AVOID THEM

L andlording is unfortunately a business that is prone to legal disputes. If you follow the advice in this book, you will minimize your chances of facing legal action. However, they will happen occasionally, and we will outline some of the most common legal issues you may face in this chapter.

One thing I have noticed over many years of being a landlord is that you will get many more verbal "threats" of legal action versus the number that will actually go to court. You will get a lot of threats from tenants saying, "I am going to take you to court," but a small percentage of them will actually file a legal action. First, because legal fights are expensive and once a tenant finds this out, they will change their mind quickly. To hire an attorney and file a legal claim will cost thousands of dollars, and quite often the disputed amount is small or just a couple hundred dollars. Second, once the other party understands that you are a professional landlord who follows the law and is more prepared than they are, the dynamic will change quickly.

The other observation is that most cases that go to court involve the landlord (plaintiff) suing a tenant or vendor (defendant) for money or removal from the apartment. It is much better to be the plaintiff versus the defendant. You still have to be prepared and prove your case, but at worst, you lose the case and maybe some court and legal fees. There is little chance for fines or penalties to be assessed as the plaintiff.

There are five key things to keep in mind regarding legal issues as a landlord:

1. Always be prepared. Have all your files and documents organized and easily located when a dispute arises.
2. Be smart. Know the local, state, and federal laws, especially regarding Fair Housing.
3. Do not be intimidated by threats of legal action. Rest assured that as a professional landlord, you will have the upper hand.
4. Never get into a verbal altercation with the other party.
5. Make sure all your communications are in writing.

By being aware of these best practices, you will avoid many of the most common legal issues landlords face. If you do end up in court, you will be prepared to win the case.

COMMON LEGAL ISSUES

Below are some of the most common legal issues you may face as a landlord. Of course, there are more, but late fee disputes, nonpayment of rent and notices of eviction, failing to return the security deposit properly, ignored repair and maintenance work, and "slip and fall" cases are the most common.

LATE FEE DISPUTES

Disputes over late fees are common and can escalate into litigation. This is why it is important to comply with state and local laws when setting and charging late fees. By doing this, you will put yourself in a strong position if and when a dispute arises. It is important to remember that excessive late fees can be invalidated by a judge.

Additionally, we recommend waiving the late payment fee on rare occasions when good tenants pay just a few days late.

NONPAYMENT OF RENT AND NOTICES OF EVICTION

A landlord can evict a tenant for the following reasons:

- Nonpayment of rent or other fees
- Failure to vacate the premises after a lease agreement has expired
- Violation of a significant provision in the lease
- Causing damage to the property

Before starting the eviction process, you must put the tenant(s) on notice that a violation has occurred and legal action could be started if they do not rectify the nonpayment within a certain time period.

Every state has different eviction regulations, but most states require a termination notice (or Notice to Quit) before filing an eviction lawsuit. Make sure you send this notice in writing, and I recommend sending it by certified mail.

FAILING TO RETURN SECURITY DEPOSITS PROPERLY

Most states have laws on how security deposits must be handled during the tenant's stay and how they must be refunded to the tenant once they move out. Be sure you know your state's laws on how and when to refund security deposits.

Most states require that security deposits are refunded with a written letter showing any deductions from the security funds. Make sure all deductions are "fair and reasonable," as some states can penalize a landlord for deductions that are deemed to have been in "bad faith."

IGNORED REPAIR AND MAINTENANCE WORK

Landlords in almost all states are required to offer and maintain rental units that meet basic health and safety standards (called the "Implied Warranty of Habitability"). If you fail to make certain repairs, deal with environmental hazards, or meet all local housing codes, a tenant may withhold rent payments until such repairs are completed.

We recommend that you ask the tenant to provide you with a list of repairs in writing, and then complete the ones that meet the habitability standard as soon as possible. Once that is done, send a demand letter to the tenant demanding payment of any unpaid rent. The eviction process can then be initiated if the rent remains unpaid.

SLIP AND FALL CASES

Many legal disputes are for relatively small dollar amounts. Experienced landlords may even choose to handle those cases independently versus hiring an attorney. However, a "slip and fall" claim from a tenant or vendor may involve a large dollar amount.

A smart landlord will hire an attorney to defend them in these cases. Oftentimes, your insurance company will be required to defend you as part of your liability insurance policy.

Once again, the theme here is to act as a professional landlord, and if you do, you will avoid most of these potential legal issues. As a landlord, you are primarily responsible for getting tenants into your property and collecting rent. You should not be dealing with legal issues on a daily basis.

WHEN TO HIRE A LAWYER

In recent years, I have not hired a lawyer very often. There is a common misconception that lawyers are the smartest people in the room, but that's not always true. As a landlord, you may have a better understanding of the unique renter–landlord relationship than anyone else. Even if the lawyer tells you the strict legal interpretation, you may be better off relying on your people skills to resolve the matter without the attorney and their fees.

In most situations where money is owed to you, I would advise that you do the math. If the tenant owes you $800 in damages, it will not be worth hiring a lawyer for $2,000 to fight the case. In that situation, your best option is to try to work something out with the tenant. Maybe you can split the difference and get $400, which is better than getting nothing. It also saves you the time and money of hiring a lawyer and pursuing the case in court.

If, however, you are being sued for a violation of Fair Housing laws or a personal injury case, you will likely need an attorney, as the cost of these issues usually warrants the hiring of professional legal counsel.

A FINAL WORD ON LEGAL ISSUES

If you are a landlord for long enough, you will encounter legal issues at some point. Handle them professionally. Never turn a discussion about money or living arrangement into something personal. When you do that, the situation becomes much more volatile and leaves you vulnerable in court. Stick to your lease, stay calm, document all communications in writing, and remain a professional landlord at all times.

Now that legal issues are out of the way, one of the last vital pieces of information for you to understand is bookkeeping, financial management, and tax issues. The mere mention of these words is often enough to scare people away, as the subjects seem overly complex. But the next chapter will familiarize you with enough basic information to feel comfortable. Do not let bookkeeping, financial management and tax issues scare you any more than legal matters. They are all well within your ability to understand as a landlord, as long as you have the necessary people skills and drive to maximize profits.

CHAPTER 14

BOOKKEEPING, FINANCIAL MANAGEMENT, AND TAX ISSUES

T he purpose of this chapter is not to make you a CPA, but to give you some basic skills and systems that will help you manage your money and taxes at a higher level. There is no point in doing all the hard work of a professional property manager only to have sloppy bookkeeping and financial management prevent you from maximizing profits. Having a foundational knowledge of bookkeeping, financial management, and tax issues is a must for a well-run property management business.

INCOME VERSUS EXPENSES

Let us start by defining bookkeeping as the recording of financial transactions, such as the income and expenses of a business. But what exactly are income and expenses?

INCOME

The money that comes into your business from your rental properties is called income. Rental property income comes in many forms, but the most common is the monthly rent. A rental property owner must record all income to be sure the financial statements and tax filings are correct. The following is a list of common incomes for a rental property owner:

- Rent
- Late fees
- Application fees
- Pet rent
- Utility payments
- NSF fees
- Interest income

One item that is not income is security deposits you hold on behalf of your tenants. Security deposits held in escrow are not considered income, except for any amount applied to repair damage or to unpaid rent after a tenant moves out.

Suppose you hold $2,000 in a security deposit, and the tenant moves out owing $500 in unpaid rent. You can keep $500 of the security deposit to offset the unpaid rent, and this amount is considered rental income and the balance would be returned to the tenant.

EXPENSES

The costs of operating your rental business are referred to as expenses. Just like income, it is critical to record all expenses in your bookkeeping system. The following is a list of many common expenses paid by a rental business:

- Maintenance and repairs
- Landscaping
- Utilities
- Advertising and marketing expenses
- Property management fees
- Accountant or attorney fees
- Rental license and business licenses
- Real estate taxes
- Insurance
- Interest on a mortgage (principal is not an expense)
- Office space and supplies
- Travel to and from your properties

This should give you a good understanding of what is considered income or an expense. Now, let us break them down further.

OPERATING VERSUS NONOPERATING ENTRIES

Both income and expenses can be further broken down into operating and nonoperating entries. The income and expenses listed previously are mostly day-to-day repeating items, which means they would be considered operating entries.

Nonoperating entries are still related to your business, but not directly to the property. For example, interest on a mortgage would be considered nonoperating, as you may or may not have interest depending on how you bought the property. Other nonoperating items might include education, such as a learning course about professional property management.

It is important to separate these items in your bookkeeping system so you can determine the normal cost to operate a building versus the cost of items that are related to running your business.

Another important reason you need to keep these categories separate is if you want to sell the property in the future. You will need to be able to show a potential buyer exactly what the true costs of the building are versus other costs that are not related to the building. You want to make it as easy as possible for your buyer to determine the income and expenses, so they can make the best offer for your property.

NET OPERATING INCOME

Net operating income (NOI) is a key measure of profitability for any business, including a rental business. It is calculated by subtracting total operating expenses from total operating revenue. It can be expressed as a dollar amount or as a percentage of total operating revenue. There are several reasons why an investor needs to know what the NOI is of each property they own.

NOI is an essential metric used to evaluate the financial performance of an investment property. Investment properties can be valued as a multiple of their NOI. In general, investors will buy investment properties that are valued at between twelve and twenty times the annual NOI. So increasing a property's NOI will result in a higher sale price. This is where many of the tools and tips in this book will help you improve your NOI and, as result, the value of your property.

The NOI is also important to real estate investors because it is used to determine the property's potential cash flow. Cash flow is the amount of money that an investor can expect to receive from the property after all expenses have been paid, and it is a critical factor in determining the profitability of a real estate investment.

After you have calculated the NOI, you can determine a property's potential sale value by calculating its cap rate. Cap rate is calculated by dividing the NOI by the property's purchase price and is used to determine the property's potential return on investment. For example, a property with an NOI of $50,000 and a purchase price of $500,000 would have a cap rate of 10%. The higher the cap rate, the more profitable the investment is and the higher the property value.

BANK ACCOUNTS

Bookkeeping and financial management require a place where you can collect your income and pay your expenses from, such as a bank account. We recommend a landlord have at least three different bank accounts to operate a rental business. These include an operating account(s), security deposit escrow, and a reserve account.

Personal versus Business Accounts

As a rental property owner, it is a best practice to never commingle your personal accounts with your business accounts. This ensures that all the income and expenses moving in and out of your business accounts never get mixed in with your personal accounts.

Additionally, this practice will make bookkeeping and tax filing much easier if you totally separate your accounts. And dedicated business bank accounts will help create a more professional image to your tenants, investors, and banker.

OPERATING ACCOUNT

The operating account is where you deposit all rent and other income. This is also the account from which you write checks and pay expenses.

If you own more than one property, you may want to have a separate operating account for each property that you own. It is not absolutely necessary, but it will make it easier when reconciling your accounts and completing tax forms.

I also recommend your operating account be with a large national bank that will integrate with your property management software.

SECURITY DEPOSIT ESCROW ACCOUNT

This account serves one purpose: to hold all your security deposit funds. Many states require landlords to keep these funds separate from their operating funds. Some states even require the landlord to pay the tenant any interest that is earned.

Security deposit escrow can be held in a traditional checking account or something that earns interest, like a money market. The only requirement is that the account must be protected by the Federal Deposit Insurance Corporation (FDIC). It is also a best practice to never put these funds into any account where the principal could be at risk, such as mutual funds or investment accounts.

RESERVE ACCOUNT

A reserve account is a checking or investment account that holds money for future large or unexpected expenses. A good example would be a roof that costs $10,000 but only occurs every fifteen years. If you build up funds in a reserve account, you will have a way to buffer your business against these unexpected or large costs.

The reserve account should be funded every month with a fixed amount (e.g., $100 per property) or a percentage of your income, such as 10%. This way, the reserve funds are constantly growing.

HOW TO TITLE BANK ACCOUNTS

If you operate your rental business in an LLC, make sure all these bank accounts are in the name of the business. This will help to make sure you do not mix your personal and business funds.

If you operate as a sole proprietor, ask your bank what options are available to title your business accounts with something other than your personal name. Something like, "Joe Smith Rental Account" should work. Another option would be to use different banks for your business and personal accounts.

BANK ACCOUNT MANAGEMENT

Reconcile these accounts at least once per month with your book-keeping system or accounting software. The purpose is to be sure your bookkeeping system and the actual bank account balances match. If there are any mistakes, they can be found quickly and corrected. I would not skip or delay this step. If you wait several months or longer to reconcile your accounts, it can be difficult to find and correct any errors.

It is also recommended that you make monthly transfers into your reserve fund. You may be able to set this up automatically each month through your online banking account.

DEPRECIATION

Depreciation expense is very important to real estate investors as it allows you to deduct the cost of the property and any improvements over the life of the property. As a result, it lowers your taxes and adds to your cash flow. But this is commonly misunderstood.

One of the primary reasons individuals buy real estate is for the tax advantages, and the depreciation allowance is probably the largest tax advantage an investor can receive. This is why wealthy individuals invest in real estate as it allows them to lower their tax bill on their other income unrelated to real estate.

A couple of points to remember about depreciation expense: First, it falls under the category of nonoperating, as described above. Second, you can depreciate the building and any improvements, but not the cost of the land.

This is not intended to be a deep discussion of how to calculate depreciation, as there are numerous ways to do it. Generally, I would recommend having your tax advisor calculate it for you. But I will provide a simplified version here, so you have a basic understanding of how depreciation works.

You need four factors in determining depreciation: the cost basis of your property, the cost of the land, any improvements, and the useful life of your property.

COST BASIS OF PROPERTY

The cost of your property is generally what you paid for it less the cost of the land. You might think, "But I do not know how much I paid for the land?" This can be tricky, but if you had an appraisal done when you purchased the property, it may separate the cost of the building and land. This would then be used as your building cost basis. If you do not have an appraisal, you may want to get one done or seek help from your tax advisor.

IMPROVEMENTS

Improvements on a property can be any money spent to upgrade the property. For example, if you put a new roof on the property at $10,000, it is considered an improvement and is added to the cost basis of the property.

USEFUL LIFE

The IRS actually simplified this in 1986 by allowing all property owners to declare 27.5 years as the useful life versus trying to determine the actual useful life.

HOW TO CALCULATE DEPRECIATION

With an understanding of cost basis, improvements, and useful life, you are ready to calculate the depreciation expense. For example, let's assume you bought a property for $200,000, of which the land was worth $40,000 and the property was valued at $160,000. You can include the closing costs and for simplicity, let's say they were $5,000. You can also add any improvements, such as the roof mentioned above for $10,000. Add these up, and the building cost basis is $175,000.

Take the cost basis of $175,000 and divide by 27.5 (the useful life of the building). This will give you the annual depreciation expense of $6,363. Enter that cost into your bookkeeping system as a nonoperating expense, and it will lower the income from this property by $6,363. If you are in the 30% tax bracket, this means a reduction in your personal taxes of $1,909 per year.

If you need more information, please consult *IRS Publication 551: Basis of Assets* for more information about how to calculate your property cost basis.

Use Cash or Accrual Method for Accounting

Another more advanced step in setting up your bookkeeping system is tracking income and expenses with a cash or accrual method of accounting. The cash method involves recording income as it is received and expenses as bills are paid. The accrual system is where you record income and expenses when they are used but not necessarily when they are paid. An example might be an insurance bill you receive in January for $1,200 for the entire year. With the cash method, you would record a $1,200 expense in January but nothing else for the rest of the year. With the accrual system, you would record $100 per month for the entire year. At the end of the year, the amounts are the same, but during the year, the balances will be different.

The pros and cons of these systems are beyond the scope of this book, but generally, landlords with fewer properties will use the cash method because it tends to be simpler. If your business grows, you may want to convert to an accrual method, as banks and outside investors tend to prefer the accrual method. The IRS only asks that you do not change systems during the year. If you want to change, do it at the end of your fiscal year.

BOOKKEEPING SYSTEMS AND SOFTWARE

Some landlords prefer to do business the old-fashioned way with paper and pencil. If you own only one or two properties, you can probably manage with this system. If you own more, you may use a spreadsheet program to track your income and expenses, which is better than paper and pencil but tends to be labor-intensive and prone to errors.

Today, the best solution for running your rental business is an accounting software package that has been designed for rental property owners. These programs have become easy to use. They track income and expenses as well as provide a system for tenants to pay online. Specialized accounting software can be set up to reconcile your bank accounts automatically and send tax forms to your vendors and contain many other features to improve your rental business.

QuickBooks and Quicken are both accounting software packages that work for just about any business. Both offer online versions for a relatively modest cost of less than $100 per month. They are designed for any business, however, so they do not have many of the features that are specialized for a professional property manager.

There are more robust packages, such as Buildium and AppFolio, which are designed specifically for property managers. They have many features that are built for landlords and tenants. If you are a landlord with only a few properties, these products might not be worth the added cost. But both products allow tenants to pay online, see their accounts and balances anytime, pay any maintenance vendors online, and they can be expanded as your rental business grows. They also allow you to send tax forms to vendors automatically.

SHOULD YOU HIRE AN ACCOUNTANT?

With the tools in this book and a good bookkeeping system or software program, most landlords will not need an accountant. Hiring an accountant can be expensive and will reduce your profits.

Still, you may want to hire an accountant at the end of each year to do a review of your records, just to be sure everything is in good order. They may find some expenses or tax deductions you missed that would reduce your tax liability. Accountants can also prepare your tax filing. This is the method I choose. We do all our day-to-day bookkeeping, but at the end of the year, I have a professional accountant review our records and prepare our taxes.

TAXES

They say the only certainties in life are death and taxes. Well, that may not be true for landlords.

If you own a rental property or several properties and collect rent and other fees, the IRS wants you to pay taxes. A nice benefit to being a landlord is that the IRS allows you to deduct many costs against your rental income and pay tax on the net profit (or loss), not the gross income.

Landlords can take advantage of certain tax deductions to reduce their taxable income. These include deductions for operating expenses, depreciation, and other costs that are directly associated with the rental of a property.

Let's take a simple example. You own a property and collect rent of $1,000 per month or $12,000 per year. You have operating expenses of $700 per month, and they include maintenance, landscaping, utilities, interest, and other normal operating costs. This means your net profit is $300 per month or $3,600 for the year. Then you can deduct the depreciation, as discussed above, of $6,363. This leaves a tax loss of $2,763. If you are in the 30% tax bracket, this tax loss will allow you to save approximately $830 per year.

This example shows how you can generate $3,600 per year in cash flow but reduce your taxes by $830 per year. This is why so many people invest in real estate, as it allows you to generate cash flow and reduce your income taxes. Now I cannot do anything about death, but we have shown that, as real estate investors, we can reduce or even eliminate your income taxes.

TAX FORMS

It is important to be aware of the different tax forms you may need to prepare and file. This topic can cover an entire book, and the information here is only scratching the surface. I still recommend hiring a certified tax accountant to file your taxes. Failing to file the correct and accurate documents can result in penalties and fines.

The IRS requires landlords to file two types of forms. First, a 1099 form that tells the IRS who you have paid, such as vendors.

Second, you need to report your income (or loss) which is done using form 1040 if you are a sole proprietor, or form 1065 if you are an LLC.

FORM 1099

The IRS mandates that you send a 1099 tax form to any person or vendor you paid over $600 for professional services during the year. This may include your landscaper, maintenance person, cleaner, or anyone else you paid $600 or more. You are not required to send a Form 1099 to corporate entities such as a utility company or your mortgage company.

Prior to hiring someone, you must collect a W-9 form. This will have their name, address, and social security number, which is what you will need to file your 1099 forms.

☐ VOID ☐ CORRECTED			
PAYER'S name, street address, city or town, state or province, country, ZIP or foreign postal code, and telephone no.	1 Rents $	OMB No. 1545-0115 Form **1099-MISC** (Rev. January 2022) For calendar year 20 ____	**Miscellaneous Information**
	2 Royalties $		
	3 Other income $	4 Federal income tax withheld $	**Copy 1** **For State Tax** **Department**
PAYER'S TIN RECIPIENT'S TIN	5 Fishing boat proceeds $	6 Medical and health care payments $	
RECIPIENT'S name	7 Payer made direct sales totaling $5,000 or more of consumer products to recipient for resale ☐	8 Substitute payments in lieu of dividends or interest $	
Street address (including apt. no.)	9 Crop insurance proceeds $	10 Gross proceeds paid to an attorney $	
City or town, state or province, country, and ZIP or foreign postal code	11 Fish purchased for resale $	12 Section 409A deferrals $	
	13 FATCA filing requirement ☐	14 Excess golden parachute payments $	15 Nonqualified deferred compensation $
Account number (see instructions)	16 State tax withheld $ $	17 State/Payer's state no.	18 State income $ $
Form **1099-MISC** (Rev. 1-2022)	www.irs.gov/Form1099MISC		Department of the Treasury - Internal Revenue Service

INDIVIDUALS/SOLE PROPRIETORS

Even though landlords are considered self-employed, they must still submit various tax forms to the IRS and other state and local tax agencies. One of the most common tax forms landlords must file is a supplemental form to your form 1040 filing called Schedule E: Supplemental Income and Loss. This form is used to report rental income and expenses. It must be filled out to report the income from your rental activities. You must include information such as the amount of rent collected, the cost of repairs and maintenance, and any other expenses related to the rental activity.

A single Schedule E form allows you to report on three properties. If you have more than three properties, you can file additional Schedule E forms to list your other properties. However, you will only fill in the "Totals" column on one Schedule E form. These totals will be the combined totals of all the Schedule E forms you file.

Another form you may need to complete as part of the form 1040 is form 4562: Depreciation and Amortization. This form is used to calculate your depreciation for the year and then is included on your Schedule E.

Form 1040 — U.S. Individual Income Tax Return

Form 1040 — Department of the Treasury—Internal Revenue Service — **U.S. Individual Income Tax Return** — **2022** — OMB No. 1545-0074 — IRS Use Only—Do not write or staple in this space.

Filing Status
Check only one box.

☐ Single ☐ Married filing jointly ☐ Married filing separately (MFS) ☐ Head of household (HOH) ☐ Qualifying surviving spouse (QSS)

If you checked the MFS box, enter the name of your spouse. If you checked the HOH or QSS box, enter the child's name if the qualifying person is a child but not your dependent:

Your first name and middle initial | Last name | Your social security number

If joint return, spouse's first name and middle initial | Last name | Spouse's social security number

Home address (number and street). If you have a P.O. box, see instructions. | Apt. no.

City, town, or post office. If you have a foreign address, also complete spaces below. | State | ZIP code

Foreign country name | Foreign province/state/county | Foreign postal code

Presidential Election Campaign
Check here if you, or your spouse if filing jointly, want $3 to go to this fund. Checking a box below will not change your tax or refund. ☐ You ☐ Spouse

Digital Assets
At any time during 2022, did you: (a) receive (as a reward, award, or payment for property or services); or (b) sell, exchange, gift, or otherwise dispose of a digital asset (or a financial interest in a digital asset)? (See instructions.) ☐ Yes ☐ No

Standard Deduction
Someone can claim: ☐ You as a dependent ☐ Your spouse as a dependent
☐ Spouse itemizes on a separate return or you were a dual-status alien

Age/Blindness You: ☐ Were born before January 2, 1958 ☐ Are blind Spouse: ☐ Was born before January 2, 1958 ☐ Is blind

Dependents (see instructions):
If more than four dependents, see instructions and check here . ☐

(1) First name Last name	(2) Social security number	(3) Relationship to you	(4) Check the box if qualifies for (see instructions): Child tax credit	Credit for other dependents
			☐	☐
			☐	☐
			☐	☐
			☐	☐

Income

Attach Form(s) W-2 here. Also attach Forms W-2G and 1099-R if tax was withheld.

If you did not get a Form W-2, see instructions.

1a	Total amount from Form(s) W-2, box 1 (see instructions)	1a	
b	Household employee wages not reported on Form(s) W-2	1b	
c	Tip income not reported on line 1a (see instructions)	1c	
d	Medicaid waiver payments not reported on Form(s) W-2 (see instructions)	1d	
e	Taxable dependent care benefits from Form 2441, line 26	1e	
f	Employer-provided adoption benefits from Form 8839, line 29	1f	
g	Wages from Form 8919, line 6	1g	
h	Other earned income (see instructions)	1h	
i	Nontaxable combat pay election (see instructions) . . 1i		
z	Add lines 1a through 1h	1z	

Attach Sch. B if required.

2a	Tax-exempt interest . . 2a		b	Taxable interest	2b	
3a	Qualified dividends . . 3a		b	Ordinary dividends	3b	
4a	IRA distributions . . 4a		b	Taxable amount .	4b	
5a	Pensions and annuities . . 5a		b	Taxable amount .	5b	
6a	Social security benefits . . 6a		b	Taxable amount .	6b	

Standard Deduction for—
- Single or Married filing separately, $12,950
- Married filing jointly or Qualifying surviving spouse, $25,900
- Head of household, $19,400
- If you checked any box under Standard Deduction, see instructions.

c	If you elect to use the lump-sum election method, check here (see instructions) . . ☐		
7	Capital gain or (loss). Attach Schedule D if required. If not required, check here . . ☐	7	
8	Other income from Schedule 1, line 10	8	
9	Add lines 1z, 2b, 3b, 4b, 5b, 6b, 7, and 8. This is your **total income**	9	
10	Adjustments to income from Schedule 1, line 26	10	
11	Subtract line 10 from line 9. This is your **adjusted gross income**	11	
12	Standard deduction or itemized deductions (from Schedule A)	12	
13	Qualified business income deduction from Form 8995 or Form 8995-A	13	
14	Add lines 12 and 13	14	
15	Subtract line 14 from line 11. If zero or less, enter -0-. This is your **taxable income**	15	

For Disclosure, Privacy Act, and Paperwork Reduction Act Notice, see separate instructions. | Cat. No. 11320B | Form **1040** (2022)

LIMITED LIABILITY CORPORATION (LLC)

If you choose to use an LLC for your rental property business, you will operate as a business versus as an individual. An LLC entity will give you added personal liability protection and a more professional business appearance.

As an LLC, you will also have flexibility in how you choose to structure your company. You can be the sole owner or you can include a spouse or other business partners in the ownership. The way your LLC's taxes are handled can vary depending on how many owners your company has and how you choose to set this up with the IRS.

If you are the only owner of the LLC, you will complete the same forms mentioned above for the sole proprietor. The IRS considers a one-person LLC essentially the same as an individual. Everything from your LLC will pass through to your personal form 1040 and Schedule E.

An LLC with multiple owners requires different tax filings. Taxes are still passed through the LLC to the owners. The LLC must complete form 1065: Return of Partnership Income (similar to form 1040 but for an LLC), and the net profits (or loss) will be included on Schedule K. Each owner will receive a separate Schedule K. They will then include the profit (or loss) on their Schedule K on their individual tax returns. This is why LLCs are called pass-through entities. All the profits or losses pass through to members and their individual filings.

The last few chapters have provided foundational knowledge on insurance, risk, legal matters, and accounting. These are all necessary aspects of being a landlord that should not take up too much of your time.

If you do not want to deal with all work involved in managing your own properties, consider hiring a professional property manager. In the final chapter, we will explore the advantages and disadvantages of self-management versus professional property management.

CHAPTER 15

SELF-MANAGEMENT VERSUS PROFESSIONAL PROPERTY MANAGEMENT

"Most entrepreneurs fail because you are working IN your business rather than ON your business."

MICHAEL GERBER, Author of *The E-Myth Revisited*

This book has given you the tools to self-manage your properties and maximize profits. If you only have a few properties, this is what most investors will do. But as you get bigger and move to five, ten, or more properties, self-management may take up too much time. In that case, you may want to consider hiring a professional property manager. Which option is best for you? By the end of this chapter, the answer should be clear.

I have seen many investors get to five or ten properties and continue to self-manage but no longer have any time to look for new deals and buy new properties. They save a few dollars but lose the ability to expand and grow their real estate business. This may not be a good trade-off.

So let us explore each option and determine which one might work best for you. As we spoke about in the introduction, even if you choose to have a professional property manager, the tools and tips in this book will serve you well in evaluating your manager.

TIME

Managing your own property takes time. You need to show vacant properties, meet vendors to set up repairs, constantly deal with tenants, collect rent, conduct inspections, resolve disputes, and many more things as part of your daily business management. If you have multiple properties, then your duties will multiply.

The advantage of self-management is that it saves money, but you need to determine if the savings are worth your time. Most real estate investors are buying real estate as an investment, not a second job. If you buy IBM stock you do not expect to have to do any work for IBM. Self-management can become a second job, as opposed to an investment.

This is where you need to determine if the extra time spent on managing your own properties is worth the money you are saving. Not to mention the time it may be taking away from your family, primary job, hobbies, and other enjoyable pastimes.

MONEY

On average, a property management firm will charge a monthly fee between 5% and 10% of your rent. They may also add extra charges for leasing vacant units, renewing leases, maintenance add-ons, obtaining your rental licenses, and other business items. All things considered, expect to pay somewhere between 10% and 15% of your monthly rent to cover their fees. But remember all these costs are tax deductible as discussed in the prior chapter.

KNOWLEDGE, EXPERTISE, AND BEST PRACTICES

As you have seen throughout this book, I have mentioned many times how important it is that you know and comply with federal, state, and local housing laws and regulations. Keeping up with these requirements can be a daunting task. Particularly when they are constantly changing as they do in Philadelphia and many other large cities.

A big advantage of having a property manager is that they have far more knowledge in these areas because they are constantly dealing with these regulations. Property managers have systems in place to ensure compliance. They are committed to understanding the ins and outs of the rental industry, including rental laws and how to avoid violating Fair Housing laws and state statutes.

STRESS

Managing your property can be stressful. Hiring a property management company can remove most of that stress by handing off the day-to-day management tasks. They will take care of repair requests, maintenance issues, working with vendors, late payments/nonpayments, and complaints, and will produce the necessary financial reports, allowing you to focus on what is important in your life.

BETTER OUTCOME FOR TENANTS

The other advantage of a property management company is they may have systems in place to improve the tenant's living experience. At my company, we offer tenants a resident benefit package that has a number of perks. These include our Zero Deposit program, where they do not have to put up a security deposit. Others include our Flex program, where a tenant can pay half their rent on the first and fifteenth of each month; a one-time waiver of a late fee; credit reporting to improve their credit scores; and many others. Individual investors generally are not going to be able to offer things like this with just a few properties.

HOW DO YOU CHOOSE A GOOD PROPERTY MANAGER?

Not all property management companies are created equal. You want to evaluate their experience, qualifications, and credentials before agreeing to work with one. The following is a list of questions you will want to ask before choosing a property management company:

- What fees do they require?
- What is their experience and how many doors do they manage?
- Do they experience a high number of evictions?
- How do they market properties?
- How quickly do they typically get new renters in a vacant property?

- What is their process for screening potential tenants?
- What process do they have in place for responding to maintenance requests?
- How do they handle late or missing rent payments?
- Can you review a sample financial statement?
- What software do they use?
- Does their agreement require a one-year commitment and are there any fees if you want to cancel?

You do not want just anyone managing your properties. Remember that your reputation as a landlord will be tied, at least in part, to the performance of your property manager. You want an experienced company that reflects your values—a place that will provide pleasant interactions with your tenants and allow you to take a more hands-off approach with your real estate investments.

Maintenance Cost

Most property management companies will require a certain dollar amount of repairs they can perform without your prior approval. This allows them to handle small repairs more quickly. For example, we ask our owners to allow us to make repairs up to $500 without their approval.

A property manager's maintenance department is a profit center. It is therefore advisable to request a copy of all invoices and review them. It is not your intention to suggest they are performing unnecessary work, but simply to ensure everything is being done correctly.

WHICH OPTION IS RIGHT FOR YOU?

Ultimately, the decision of whether to self-manage or hire a professional property management company depends on your individual goals and circumstances. You now have all the tools to handle the tasks associated with managing your own properties. On the other hand, if you value expertise and are willing to pay for the convenience of having someone else handle the day-to-day tasks for you, hiring a professional property management company may be a better choice.

As Michael Gerber said in his book *The E-Myth Revisited*, a business owner needs to learn the skill of working ON your business versus working IN your business. Hiring a property manager is essentially the same thing, allowing you to work on your business, not in your business.

NEXT STEPS

Congratulations, and thank you for reading *Landlord Secrets*. I hope this book has provided you with the tools and tips you were looking for to own and manage your real estate investments. My goal was to make it easier for landlords to manage their properties and to maximize profits.

Please feel free to contact me at MLautensack@delvalproperty .com if you have any questions.

SAMPLE LEASE

PLAIN LANGUAGE LEASE

If you do not meet your Lease obligations, you may lose your security deposit(s). You may also be evicted and sued for monetary damages. Please read the LEASE slowly and carefully and ask about anything you do not understand.

The Landlord and Resident agree to lease the house/apartment on the following terms:

LANDLORD:

RESIDENT(S):

If more than one resident signs this lease, each resident is responsible individually and together for the full rent payment and all other utilities and fees. For example, if one resident moves out, Landlord can make the remaining Residents responsible to pay the full rent and utilities. It also means Landlord can sue either Resident for breaking the Lease.

ADDRESS FOR NOTICES AND RENT PAYMENTS:

1) **ADDRESS OF LEASED UNIT:**

2) **TERM:** The initial term ("Initial Term") of this Lease is _____ months starting _____ through _____. If neither party elects to terminate this Lease at the end of the Initial Term this lease will automatically renew on a month-to-month basis ("Renewal Term").

3) **MONTHLY RENT:** The Resident agrees to pay **$0,000.00** for the period of _____ through _____, and **$0,000.00** per month for each remaining month of the Initial Term. All rent is to be paid in advance of the first *(1st)* day of each month for the Initial Term of this Lease. If the Monthly Rent has not been received by the fifth *(5th)* day of each month, then a 5-day Notice-to-Quit (NTQ) may be posted to pay all outstanding rent or vacate the Leased Unit. **Unless otherwise notified in writing, the Monthly Rent shall increase by ten percent (10%) upon completion of the Initial Term.**

Initial _____ **Initial** _____

4) **MOVE-IN COSTS:**

	Amount	Charge
First Month Rent	$0000.00	Monthly
Last Month Rent	$0000.00	Monthly
Pet Rent	N/A	Monthly
Security Deposit	$0000.00	Refundable deposit
Key Deposit	$25.00	Refundable deposit
Additional Deposit	$00.00	See attached Pet Addendum
Total Due	$0000.00	

5) **PET RENT:** Resident agrees to pay **$00** per month for each month of the Initial Term, or any future Renewal Terms as Pet Rent.

Initial _____ **Initial** _____

6) **ADDITIONAL RENT:** Additional Rent is charged for late payments, any payment returned for insufficient funds, and other charges as outlined below.
- **LATE FEE:** If any or all of the Monthly Rent or Pet Rent is not received by the fifth *(5th)* day of a month, the Monthly Rent shall increase by $75.00 for that particular month.
- **RETURNED CHECK FEE:** There is a $25.00 returned check charge for any payment returned for insufficient funds. In the event that two of the Resident's checks are dishonored during any twelve *(12)* month

period, the Resident shall be required to make all future payments via money order or cashier's check.

- **NOTICE TO QUIT:** If the landlord sends a 5-day Notice-to-Quit an additional $25 will be charged.
- **HOLDOVER FEE:** Resident(s) shall have no right to holdover possession of the Leased Unit after the expiration or termination of this Lease without Landlord's prior written consent, which consent may be withheld in Landlord's sole and absolute discretion. If Resident(s) retain possession of any part of the Leased Unit after the Initial Term or future Renewal Terms, Resident(s) shall become a month-to-month resident for the entire Lease Unit upon all of the terms of this Lease as might be applicable to such month-to-month tenancy, except that Resident(s) shall pay Monthly Rent at 150% of the rate in effect immediately prior to such holdover plus pay a Holdover Fee of $50 per day.

7) **ORDER IN WHICH RENT PAYMENTS ARE APPLIED:** Landlord applies all monies received in the following order:

1. Late Rent and any Late Rent Fees, Returned Check Fees and Notice to Quit Fees
2. Legal and/or court fees
3. Resident-owed utility bills
4. Any other fees owed but not paid
5. Past rent then Current rent

8) **SECURITY DEPOSIT:** Resident has delivered to Landlord a security deposit of **$000.00** as security that Resident will perform their obligations under this Lease. Landlord may use any portion of the security deposit to pay for loss or damages due to Resident's breach of this Lease or for any damages to the Leased Unit. Any loss or damage not covered by the security deposit shall be payable by Resident as additional rent. Resident may not apply the security deposit toward the rent for the Leased Unit. Landlord may retain the security deposit if Resident fails to make full rental payments as required by this Lease, or if Resident vacates prior to the end of the Lease Term. Landlord shall deposit

the security deposit at First Trust. To be eligible for return of the security deposit after vacating the Leased Unit, Resident must comply with all elements of the **Security Deposit Refund Addendum (Attachment #5)**.

9) **UTILITIES: All utilities shall be at Resident's expense. Resident agrees that these utilities shall be placed in the name of Resident on or before the move-in date and all utilities shall be promptly paid when due.**

10) **PEST CONTROL:** During the first 30 days of tenancy, the Landlord is responsible for pest control if reported by Resident. Resident is solely responsible for any pest removal needed following the first 30 days of tenancy.

11) **USE AND OCCUPANCY OF PREMISES:**
   a. Resident will personally use and continuously occupy the Leased Unit as a private dwelling for Resident and Resident's immediate family or co-residents consisting of the following person(s):
   Additional Resident: _____
   Additional Resident: _____
   It is a breach of this Lease to have any person(s) residing in the Leased Unit who is not listed in this Paragraph. The resident who signs this Lease agrees and warrants that he or she has authority to sign for all additional resident(s).
   b. Resident will not remove or attempt to remove Resident's personal property from the Leased Unit without first paying to Landlord all rent due for the balance of the term of this Lease.
   c. Resident will notify Landlord if Resident intends to be away from the Unit for more than ten (10) days.
   d. Resident will comply with all relevant statutes, laws, ordinances, and regulations. Resident will not keep anything in the Leased Unit or conduct any activity, which is dangerous or might increase the danger to the Leased Unit or to other occupants in the building.
   e. Resident will not act in any way which unreasonably disturbs the peace and quiet of other residents.

12) **POSSESSION:** Landlord will make a good faith effort to make the Leased Unit available to Resident on the day this Lease is scheduled to begin. If any delay does occur, no rent will be due until the Leased Unit is made available to Resident. This Lease will be terminated at Resident's written request and acceptance by Landlord if the Leased Unit is not available within ten (10) days after the date this Lease is scheduled to begin. Termination of the Lease by Resident is Resident's only remedy. Landlord will not be responsible for any inconvenience, loss, or damage in the event of any delay in making the Leased Unit available to Resident. All Residents' deposits held by Landlord will be refunded.

13) **SUBLETTING:** Resident may **not** sublease or assign this Lease or sublease the Leased Unit. Resident may not permit the Leased Unit to be occupied by any person other than those in Paragraph 11(a).

14) **ALTERATIONS:** Resident may not under any conditions change locks without first obtaining Landlord's written permission. Resident may not paint, remodel, or make any structural changes to the interior or exterior of the Leased Unit, or attach or remove any carpeting or fixtures without first obtaining Landlord's written permission. When this Lease terminates, the Lease Unit must be returned to the original condition.

15) **CONDITION OF LEASED UNIT; REPAIR OF DAMAGE:** Resident has examined the Leased Unit and is satisfied with its present physical condition. Resident agrees to maintain the Leased Unit during the term of this Lease, and to return possession of the Leased Unit at the end of the term of this Lease, in the same condition as it is on the date of this Lease, except for ordinary wear and tear. If the Leased Unit is damaged or repairs are required Resident will promptly notify Landlord in writing. Landlord agrees to perform the repairs with reasonable promptness after written notice from Resident, and to pay for repairs required due to ordinary wear and tear. Resident agrees to pay as Additional Rent the cost of the repair of damage caused by Resident or other permitted occupants or visitors of Resident. No repairs to the Leased Unit may be made by anyone except Landlord's employees, agents, or contractors. Landlord is

not responsible for any inconvenience or loss due to necessary repairs to the Leased Unit, interruption of any utility services, or for any other reason beyond Landlord's control.

Resident is required to fill in Move-in Checklist and send to Del Val office within seven (7) days of the move-in date. **If the Checklist is not received within that time, Del Val considers the Leased Unit accepted as satisfactory by Resident.**

Initial _____ Initial _____

16) **DISASTERS:** Landlord is not responsible for any personal property damages due to the loss/failure of electricity, gas, heat, water, refrigeration, telephone, sewer, or any other public or privately supplied utility or service because of conditions beyond the control of the Landlord. This includes both Acts of God and man-made failures and shortcomings. Resident also agrees to permit Landlord to temporarily turn off utilities for required maintenance.

17) **CASUALTY:** There will be no abatement of Rent in the event of fire or other casualty. However, if in Landlord's judgment the Leased Unit becomes uninhabitable due to damage by fire or other casualty not caused by Resident or other permitted occupants of the Leased Unit or their visitors, this Lease will terminate when Resident pays all rent due to the date that Resident vacates the Leased Unit. Landlord is not responsible for any loss, damage, or inconvenience sustained by Resident due to fire or other casualty.

18) **RESIDENT'S PERSONAL PROPERTY AND INSURANCE: Landlord will not be responsible for any damage to Resident's personal property. For that reason, Resident must obtain insurance to protect his or her personal property. It will be considered a breach of this Lease to fail to obtain personal property insurance.** Any personal property left in the Leased Unit after Resident has vacated or has been evicted shall be considered abandoned, and Landlord may dispose of it in any manner without notice to Resident. Landlord's cost of disposal shall be payable by Resident as Additional Rent.

Initial _____ Initial _____

19) **ACCESS:** Landlord, Owner, or anyone authorized by Landlord may enter the Leased Unit after first notifying Resident 24 hours prior to entering. In the event of any emergency, Landlord may enter the Leased Unit without giving Resident advance 24-hour notice. Landlord may enter Leased Unit at any time to inspect with 24-hour notice to repair and maintain Leased Unit, or to show the Leased Unit to any prospective buyer, financing agent, or insurance agent, and in case either party has given notice of termination of the Leased Unit, to show the unit to any prospective resident.

20) **YARD MAINTENANCE AND SNOW REMOVAL:** Resident shall be responsible for all yard maintenance and snow removal at the Leased Unit. If the Landlord receives fines or violations from Code Enforcement or other authorities related to failure to perform lawn maintenance or remove snow, Resident will be responsible for all fines and penalties.

21) **PETS: No** pets are permitted. Resident must notify landlord of any pets inhabiting the property. This notification must be made in writing and is subject to the Landlord's approval and may require an additional security deposit. See Pet Addendum (Attachment #3). Resident(s) also agrees to pay a **$250.00** assessment, per occurrence, for an unauthorized pet in the Leased Unit.

22) **STORAGE AND PARKING:** Unless otherwise provided in this Lease, the designated storage and parking areas, if applicable, may be used by Resident at no cost, but only as Landlord may from time to time direct for the common convenience of all residents. Landlord shall not be liable for any damage to stored goods or parked vehicles resulting from the acts of person other than Landlord. Landlord shall be entitled to discontinue providing storage and parking areas at any time, in which event Resident shall immediately remove all goods and vehicles as Landlord may direct. Resident's failure to remove such goods and vehicles shall constitute Resident's appointment of Landlord as Resident agent to a public warehouse at Resident's own risk and cost, and Landlord shall not be liable for any resulting loss, damage, or injury to persons or property. The parking areas may be used only to park operable automobiles and such other types of noncommercial vehicles as Landlord may approve. All other vehicles will be towed at the owner's expense.

23) **LEASE TERMINATION OR RENEWAL:**

   a. Either Landlord or Resident may terminate this Lease at the end of the Initial Term or any renewal term by written notice, which must be received at least thirty (30) days prior to the end of the Term.

   b. If neither party elects to terminate at the end of the Initial Term this lease will automatically renew on a month-to-month basis.

   c. Landlord may increase the rent or change the Term of the Lease for any renewal period by sending written notice to Resident at least thirty (30) days before the end of the Initial Term or of any Renewal Term. Resident may reject the renewal terms by sending written notice to Landlord within thirty (30) days of the date of Landlord's renewal notice and shall vacate at the end of the Initial Term. If Resident does not send notice terminating the Lease, it shall renew on the terms set forth in Section 2 of this Lease Agreement.

   d. If Landlord does not agree in writing to Resident's request to terminate this Lease before the end of the Initial Term or of any Renewal Term, Resident will be responsible for all costs and losses incurred by Landlord due to such early termination, including but not limited to any loss of rent for the balance of the Lease Term, any costs for preparing the Leased Unit for re-renting, and any commissions to re-rent the property.

24) **LANDLORD'S REMEDIES:** If at any time Resident fails to make any rent payment within five (5) days after it is due or fails to comply with any other provision of this Lease, Landlord may take any or all of the following actions. Landlord may exercise any or all of these remedies which shall not prevent Landlord from exercising that remedy or any other remedies at the same time or at any other time:

   • Landlord may declare all rents for the balance of the Initial Term or any Renewal Term of this Lease to be immediately due and payable by Resident, and Landlord may sue to collect this rent.

   • Landlord may terminate this Lease.

   • Landlord may evict Resident.

- Landlord may sue Resident to collect any sums owed by Resident under this Lease including but not limited to reasonable legal fees, an Eviction Processing Fee of $250, and court costs to enforce lease terms. Resident agrees to pay all reasonable legal fees and court costs.
- Landlord may exercise any one or more of the other remedies available to it under law or in equity.
- Landlord's shall be entitled to the costs of enforcing this Lease and collecting any amounts due including reasonable legal fees, an Eviction Processing Fee of $250, and court costs to enforce lease terms.

25) NOTICE TO LEAVE THE LEASED UNIT (NOTICE TO QUIT): If Resident breaks this Lease, Resident agrees to give up his/her right of a "Notice to Quit." This means Resident allows Landlord to go to Court without giving the required notice.

Initial _____ Initial _____

26) VACATING LEASED UNIT: At the time that Resident vacates the Leased Unit, Resident must notify the Landlord and must return all keys.

27) LOCKS and KEYS: Landlord will provide keys to the front and back entrance doors and if applicable any mailboxes of the property. Under no circumstances should Residents change the locks. If locked out of the Property, Resident will pay Landlord a $75 fee to unlock door. If the keys are lost and locks must be changed, Resident will pay Landlord a $125 fee to change the locks.

28) NO WAIVER BY LANDLORD: If at any time Landlord does not exercise any of its rights under this Lease, Landlord does not forfeit its right to exercise them at a later date. Acceptance of past due rent is not a waiver of Landlord's right to enforce this Lease.

29) RELEASE OF LANDLORD: Landlord shall not be responsible for any injury, property damage, or loss sustained by Resident or any other person on or in connection with the Leased Unit or Property. Resident agrees to release Landlord of responsibility for any damage, loss, or injury caused by any other person occupying the Leased Unit, or Landlord or Landlord's agents or employees which results from any of their acts or failure to act. All claims against Landlord for any damage, loss, or injury are hereby expressly waived by Resident.

30) **APPLICATION:** Landlord may terminate this Lease if any of the information provided by Resident in its Rental Application for this Lease was inaccurate.

31) **ADDITIONAL TERMS AND CONDITIONS:** Additional terms and conditions of this Lease are set forth in the "Rules and Regulations" (Attachment #1) which are attached to and are a part of this Lease. Violation of any of the "Rules and Regulations" is a breach of this Lease.

32) **SEPARABILITY:** If one or more of the provisions of this Lease is determined to be invalid, the remainder of this Lease shall remain in effect.

33) **REPORT TO CREDIT/RESIDENT AGENCIES:** You are hereby notified that a nonpayment, late payment, or breach of any of the terms of this Lease may be submitted/reported to a credit and/or resident reporting agency, and may create a negative credit record on your credit report.

34) **LEAD NOTIFICATION REQUIREMENT:** For rental dwellings built before 1978, Resident acknowledges receipt of the following: See Attachment #4.

35) **LEASE CHANGES:** The terms and conditions of this Lease may only be changed if in writing and signed by both Landlord and Resident. No oral changes or agreements are permitted.

36) **Attached are riders, addenda, and amendments—Schedule A**
   a. Attachment No. 1: Rules and Regulations.
   b. Attachment No. 2: Drug-Free Housing Addendum.
   c. Attachment No. 3: Pet Addendum.
   d. Attachment No. 4: Lead-Based Paint Notification.
   e. Attachment No. 5: Security Deposit Refund Procedure.
   f. Attachment No. 6: Remediation of Mold Addendum.
   g. Attachment No. 7: Rent Collection Policy & Procedure.
   h. Attachment No. 8: Move-In/Move-out Inspection Form.

RULES AND REGULATIONS

Referred to in the Foregoing Lease and Made Part Thereof

1. Not to obstruct the sidewalks, corridors, walls, passages, stairways, common areas, or any other place in the building of which the Leased Unit is a part, with goods, carriages, bicycles, or anything else.
2. Not to exhibit his/her name anywhere except in the place provided for such purpose by Landlord.
3. Not to keep any animals in or about the Leased Unit or the building of which it is a part.
4. Not to do anything that will interfere with the comfort or convenience of other residents.
5. Not to bring or keep in the Leased Unit anything which would in any way increase the rate of fire insurance or do anything which conflicts with the rules and ordinances of the municipality, or to commit any illegal or unlawful act in, upon, or about said building and Leased Unit.
6. Not to injure, deface, or damage any wall, ceiling, floor, woodwork, wiring fixture, plumbing, appliance, and/or part of any equipment in the Leased Unit and/or building of which it is a part.
7. Not to make any alterations, additions, or improvements without the written consent of Landlord. Any alterations, additions, or improvements so made shall become the property of Landlord.
8. Not to bring into or keep any explosive substances upon the Leased Unit and/or building of which it is a part.

9. To dispose of garbage and other refuse and/or waste matter in such place and in such manner as the Landlord or his agent may direct.

10. Not to play televisions, radios, CD players, pianos, or other musical instruments loudly after 10 p.m. or before 7:30 a.m.

11. Not to shake out of any window or hang out there any carpet, rug, or any other article; nor to sweep any dirt and other substance into any of the corridors leading from said Leased Unit, or fire tower.

12. Not to use any window shades or awnings that are not approved by Landlord.

13. To accept, as binding upon him/her, any notice which, in the judgment of Landlord, may be necessary for the safety, care, and/or cleanliness of the Leased Unit or of the building and for the preservation of good order therein; such notice when communicated in writing to Resident shall form part of this lease.

14. Not to erect any outside aerials in connection with any radio or satellite installation without the written consent.

15. Not to add and/or change any locks without the written consent of Landlord.

16. Not to use the Leased Unit for disorderly and/or immoral purposes, and/or in violation of any Federal, State, or Local Laws in force or which may be hereafter enacted relating to the manufacture, possession, storage, or sale of intoxicating substances.

SPECIAL CLAUSES—PART II

A. RESIDENT understands that if any or all of the rent is not received by the 5th of a month, Resident shall pay Late Fee of Seventy-Five Dollars ($75.00).

B. RESIDENT agrees not to place waterbeds in the Leased Unit.

C. RESIDENT agrees to abide by all borough or township codes or shall be held directly responsible for violation of same.

D. RESIDENT agrees to report immediately by phone and in writing any leaks in plumbing, heating system, or roof, or shall be held responsible for any resulting damages or expenses.

E. RESIDENT agrees not to use any kerosene heaters or to store any flammable liquids on Leased Unit.

F. LANDLORD warrants that all drain and sewer lines are clear and free at the time of occupancy and RESIDENT agrees that it is his/her responsibility to keep these drains clear.

G. RESIDENT agrees that it is his/her responsibility to obtain insurance covering his/her own personal goods and property against any loss and/or damage.

H. RESIDENT agrees that in the event of eviction proceedings, resident will pay all reasonable legal fees, an Eviction Processing Fee of $250, and court costs to enforce lease terms.

I. RESIDENT agrees that this is a NONSMOKING unit.

Initial _____ **Initial** _____

_____   _____

Landlord   Date

_____   _____

Resident   Date

_____   _____

Resident   Date

DRUG-FREE HOUSING ADDENDUM

IN CONSIDERATION of the execution or renewal of the Lease of the dwelling unit identified in the Lease, Landlord and Resident agree as follows:

1. Resident, any member of resident's household, or a guest or other person under the resident's control shall not engage in criminal activity, including drug-related criminal activity, on or near project premises. "Drug-related criminal activity" means the illegal manufacture, sale, distribution, use, or possession with intent to manufacture, see, distribute, or use, of a controlled substance (as defined in Section 102 of the Controlled Substances Act [21 U.S.C. 802]).

2. Resident, any member of resident's household, or a guest or other person under the resident's control shall not engage in any act intended to facilitate criminal activity, including drug-related criminal activity, on or near project premises.

3. Resident or members of the household will not permit the dwelling unit to be used for, or to facilitate, criminal activity, including drug-related criminal activity or possession of drug paraphernalia, regardless of whether the individual engaging in such activity is a member of the household or a guest.

4. Resident or member of the household will not engage in the manufacture, sale, or distribution of illegal drugs at any location, whether on or near project premises or otherwise.

5. Resident, any member of the resident's household, or a guest or other person under the resident's control shall not engage in acts of violence or threats of violence, including, but not limited to, the unlawful discharge of firearms, on or near project premises.

6. VIOLATION OF THE ABOVE PROVISIONS SHALL BE A MATERIAL VIOLATION OF THE LEASE AND GOOD CAUSE FOR TERMINATION OF TENANCY. A single violation of any of the provisions of this addendum shall be deemed a serious violation and a material noncompliance with the lease. It is understood and agreed that a single violation shall be good cause for termination of the lease. Unless otherwise provided by law, proof of violation shall not require criminal conviction, but shall be by a preponderance of the evidence.

7. In case of conflict between the provisions of this addendum and any other provisions of the lease, the provisions of the addendum shall govern.

8. This Lease Addendum is incorporated into the lease executed or renewed this day between Owner and Resident.

BY SIGNATURE BELOW, the resident agrees to the terms and conditions contained in this Lease Addendum.

_____	_____
Landlord	Date
_____	_____
Resident	Date
_____	_____
Resident	Date

PET ADDENDUM

THIS ADDENDUM to the Lease Agreement between Landlord and Resident entered into on _____, constitutes Attachment No. 3 to the Lease Agreement.

WITNESSETH:

WHEREAS, Resident desires and has received permission from the Landlord to keep the pet(s) named _____ and described as _____; and

WHEREAS, this Pet Addendum with Pet Policy becomes Attachment No. 3 to and part of the Lease between Landlord and Resident.

IT IS AGREED that the Landlord may revoke permission for Resident to keep said Pet on the premises by giving Resident proper written notice. Failure to comply on the part of the Resident will be deemed *"Material Noncompliance"* of the Lease and will be grounds for eviction. In the event of default by Resident of any of the terms of this Addendum, Resident agrees, upon proper written notice of default from Landlord, to cure the default, remove the Pet, or vacate the premises.

IT IS FURTHER AGREED that the Resident will pay the Landlord a Pet Security Deposit in the amount of $300.00 (refundable). The Pet Security Deposit is due and payable on or before the move-in date. The Pet Security Deposit under this Pet Addendum with Pet Policy does not limit the Resident's liability for property damages, cleaning, deodorization, defleaing, replacements, and/or personal injuries as herein further specified. The Resident's liability applies to but is not limited to carpets, doors, walls, drapes, windows, screens, furniture, appliances, and any other part of the dwelling unit, landscaping, or other improvements to the Owner's property. Resident shall be strictly liable for the entire amount of any damages to the premises or property if damages caused by said pet(s). The Resident shall indemnify Owner and Landlord from all costs of litigation and attorney fees resulting from same.

IT IS FURTHER AGREED that the Resident shall have all carpeting professionally cleaned prior to vacating the dwelling and that the Resident shall provide the Landlord with the carpet cleaning company's invoice detailing that all carpeting has been cleaned.

IT IS FURTHER AGREED that the Resident will comply with the State and local governments' Health and Safety Codes; and all other applicable governmental laws and regulations such as but not limited to licensing and keeping pet leashed while walking outside, if applicable, etc. The Resident further represents that the Pet is quiet and housebroken and will not cause any damage or annoyance to other Residents. Resident shall not permit the pet to cause any damage, discomfort, annoyance, nuisance, or in any way to inconvenience other Residents thereby resulting in complaints from any other Resident.

IT IS FURTHER AGREED that the pet will not be permitted outside the Resident's unit, if applicable, **unless the pet(s) is/are carried in Resident's arms until the building has been exited**. No pets are permitted to walk in any common corridors, elevators, community rooms, laundry rooms, or offices. Use of the grounds or premises of Landlord for sanitary purposes is prohibited. Violation of this regulation will result in one (1) formal written warning of the violation. A small section of the grounds where available will be set aside for exercise and normal body functions but **it is the pet owner's responsibility to clean up completely behind his/her pet**.

IT IS FURTHER AGREED that any pet(s) left unattended for twelve (12) hours or more or whose health is jeopardized by the Resident's neglect, mistreatment, or inability to care for the pet shall be reported to the SPCA or other appropriate authority. Such circumstances shall be deemed an emergency for the purposes of the Landlord's right to enter the Resident's unit in order to allow such authority to remove the pet from the premises. **The Owner and Landlord accept no responsibility for any pet so removed.**

IT IS FURTHER AGREED that Resident will indemnify, defend and hold harmless Owner, Landlord, their employees, and invitees from and against any and all claims, actions, suits, judgments, and demands brought by any other party because of or in connection with any activity of or damage caused by the Resident's pet.

IT IS FURTHER AGREED that Resident acknowledges that three *(3)* violations of this Addendum will be considered "*Material Noncompliance*" of this Pet Addendum and is considered grounds for termination of same.

IN WITNESS WHEREOF, the parties hereto, intending to be legally bound hereby, have executed this Pet Addendum with Pet Policy and Rules as Attachment No. 3 of the Lease Agreement as of the day and year first above written.

_____   _____
Landlord   Date

_____   _____
Resident   Date

_____   _____
Resident   Date

DISCLOSURE OF INFORMATION ON LEAD-BASED PAINT AND/OR LEAD-BASED PAINT HAZARDS LEASE ADDENDUM

LEAD WARNING STATEMENT: *Housing built before 1978 may contain lead-based paint. Lead from paint, paint chips, and dust can pose health hazards if not managed properly. Lead exposure is especially harmful to young children and pregnant women. Before renting pre-1978 housing, lessors must disclose the presence of known lead-based paint and/or lead-based paint hazards in the dwelling. Lessees must also receive a federally approved pamphlet on lead poisoning prevention.*

LESSOR'S DISCLOSURE (Initial)

_____ (a) Presence of lead-based paint or lead-based paint hazards (check one below):

    _____ Known lead-based paint and/or lead-based paint hazards are present in the housing.

    _____ Lessor has no knowledge of lead-based paint or paint hazards in housing.

_____ (b) Records and reports available to the lessor (check one below):

_____ Lessor has provided the lessee with all available records and reports pertaining to lead-based paint and/or lead-based paint hazards in the housing (list documents below).

_____ Lessor has no reports or records pertaining to lead-based paint and/or lead-based paint hazards in the housing.

LESSEE'S ACKNOWLEDGMENT (Initial)

_____ (c) Lessee has received copies of all information listed above.

_____ (d) Lessee has received *Protect Your Family from Lead in Your Home*.

AGENT'S ACKNOWLEDGMENT (Initial)

_____ (e) Agent has informed the lessor of the lessor's obligations under 42 U.S.C. 4852d and is aware of his/her responsibility to ensure compliance.

The following parties have reviewed the information above and certify, to the best of their knowledge, that the information provided by the signatory is true and accurate.

_____	_____
Landlord	Date
_____	_____
Resident	Date
_____	_____
Resident	Date

SECURITY DEPOSIT REFUND PROCEDURE

The following are the requirements that must be met if you are to receive a refund (full or partial) of your Security Deposit.

1. A written thirty *(30)* day Notice to Vacate must be provided to the Landlord. If you do not give the full thirty *(30)* day notice before lease termination date, the lease will automatically renew on a month-to-month basis and notice must be given 30 days prior to end of month of lease extension.
2. All rents and/or charges must be paid in full.
3. All keys must be returned to the Landlord. Rent will be charged until all keys are returned or unit returned to Landlord through the Courts.
4. Your apartment must be left in a clean condition. You must clean the stove, exhaust range hood, refrigerator, all other appliances, bathroom fixtures, cabinets, and remove all trash and personal items.*
5. You will be charged for damage beyond normal wear and tear to the apartment. This includes missing items such as: light bulbs, drip pans, toilet paper holders, screens, doorknobs, etc.*
6. Forwarding address must be given at the time of move-out. Failure to supply Landlord with a forwarding address at the time of move-out may result in your Security Deposit not being sent in a timely manner.

7. In the case of eviction, you will automatically forfeit your entire Security Deposit and will be billed for all necessary painting and cleaning damages beyond normal wear and tear, keys not returned, etc.

*See Attachment #8 for specific instructions.

If the above requirements are met, your Security Deposit will be refunded within thirty *(30)* days after the apartment has been vacated. You have the right to dispute any charges made against your Security Deposit within thirty *(30)* days of receipt of those charges. If charges exceed the amount of your Security Deposit, you will be billed for those charges; and Landlord will send your file to a collection agency and the Credit Bureau if account is not paid in full within the required time frame stated in said notice of outstanding charges.

_____   _____

Landlord   Date

_____   _____

Resident   Date

_____   _____

Resident   Date

REMEDIATION OF MOLD

RESIDENT AGREES to use his/her best efforts to prevent any conditions including excessive moisture that could or would create an opportunity for the growth of mold. If resident allows such conditions to develop, he/she agrees to correct such conditions.

LANDLORD will not be responsible for any conditions allowed or caused by Resident's conduct that leads to or aggravates the growth of mold. Resident will indemnify and hold Landlord harmless from any such conduct of the Resident.

RESIDENT AGREES to promptly report to Management, in writing, any actual or potential mold problems regardless of their cause. Failure to make such a written report will constitute a breach and unconditional waiver and release of any and all claims for any relief, including any alleged damages whether accrued, contingent, suspected or unsuspected, related to or occurring from or out of the unreported conditions.

IN THE EVENT Landlord notifies Resident that the Landlord intends to remediate the mold in the Resident's unit, the Resident will give immediate access to the Landlord to the unit. Should Landlord determine that the Resident must vacate the unit during the remediation, Resident will relocate at Landlord's expense to another unit within the Community while the remediation takes place. If there is no unit in the Community available, Landlord shall provide Resident at Landlord's discretion either:

1. Relocation at Landlord's expense to another nearby Community owned or managed by the Landlord or Management Company; or

2. Termination of the Lease Agreement without penalty or any financial obligation beyond the date of such termination.

Should the Resident refuse to relocate in accordance with these provisions or interfere with the Landlord's remediation efforts, said action shall constitute a breach of the Lease Agreement and an unconditional waiver and release of any and all claims for any relief, including any alleged damages, whether accrued, contingent, or otherwise, or occurring or arising from or out of exposure to the presence of mold.

LANDLORD may terminate the Lease Agreement and/or evict Resident immediately upon the Resident's breach of any provision of this Addendum. Landlord may exercise any one or more of any other remedy available to Landlord under the terms of the Lease Agreement for a breach or at law remedy available to Landlord under the terms of the Lease Agreement for a breach or at law or in equity.

IF the Resident has presented the Landlord with a written report of an actual mold problem in the unit and IF the Landlord has not within five (5) days inspected said unit or begun remediating the mold in the Resident's unit or has not provided the Resident with a Plan of Action for the remediation of the mold in the Resident's unit, the Resident may terminate the Lease Agreement without penalty for such termination and without any financial obligation beyond the date of such termination.

NOTHING in this Addendum shall release the Resident from any obligations or claims related to delinquent and/or past due rent and/or other fees or charges or other amounts due and owing including, without limitation, rent and utility or other similar fees prorated to the date of such termination.

EXCEPT AS SPECIFICALLY STATED HEREIN, all other terms and conditions of the Lease Agreement shall remain unchanged and the provisions of the Lease Agreement shall be applicable to the fullest extent not inconsistent with this Addendum. In the event of any conflict between the terms of this Addendum and the terms of the Lease Agreement, the terms of this Addendum shall control.

IN WITNESS WHEREOF, the parties hereto, intending to be legally bound hereby, have executed this Remediation of Mold as Attachment No. 6 of the Lease Agreement as of the day and year first above written.

_____   _____
Landlord   Date

_____   _____
Resident   Date

_____   _____
Resident   Date

RENT COLLECTION POLICY AND PROCEDURE

ALL RENT PAYMENTS ARE TO BE MADE PAYABLE TO:

xxxxxx

DELIVERED BY MAIL TO:

xxxxxxxxxxxxxxxxx

PAID ELECTRONICALLY:
Resident shall provide Landlord with e-mail address and will receive instructions on how to access our property management software and pay your Monthly Rent through an online electronic transfer.

RENT IS DUE ON OR BEFORE THE FIRST DAY OF EACH MONTH. **ALL RENT PAYMENTS MUST BE PAID IN FULL.** RENT IS CONSIDERED LATE ON THE FIFTH DAY OF EACH MONTH. ANY RESIDENT PAYING RENT AFTER THE FIFTH DAY OF THE MONTH WILL PAY A LATE CHARGE OF $75.00. ON THE 10th DAY OF EACH MONTH, A **NOTICE TO PAY OR QUIT** WILL BE SERVED. IF RENT IS NOT PAID WITHIN THE TIME STATED ON SAID NOTICE, EVICTION PROCEEDINGS MAY BEGIN.

IF THE RESIDENT IS UNABLE TO PAY THE RENT BY THE FIRST OF THE MONTH PLEASE E-MAIL OR CALL TO EXPLAIN WHY YOUR RENT IS LATE AND WHEN MANAGEMENT CAN EXPECT TO RECEIVE PAYMENT.

ALL RENT MUST BE PAID BY PERSONAL CHECK, ONLINE, CASHIER'S CHECK, OR MONEY ORDER. NO CASH IS ACCEPTED AT ANY TIME. CASHIER'S CHECK OR MONEY ORDER IS REQUIRED TO CURE ANY PAY OR QUIT NOTICE.

RESIDENT AGREES TO BE LIABLE FOR ALL COSTS OF COLLECTION INCLUDING ATTORNEY'S FEES, AN EVICTION PROCESSING FEE, AND COURT COST.

MOVE-OUT CLEANING INSTRUCTIONS

**ALL ITEMS MUST BE COMPLETED FOR
RETURN OF SECURITY DEPOSIT**

**THIS FORM MUST BE FAXED TO OUR OFFICE AT 610-500-5682
AND KEYS LEFT ON KITCHEN COUNTER**

We are aware that moving sometimes creates a chaotic situation and you may forget to do some of the things required under your Lease when moving out. For this reason, we submit this procedure form to assist you. We hope this list will help you prepare to vacate the unit. Please refer to the "Charges upon Termination" form that you signed. Check off the following items when completed.

1. Stove will be thoroughly cleaned by <u>removal of all grease</u> from the burners, including the <u>area under the burners</u> which can be accessed by lifting up the stove top; oven including the broiling pan area <u>under the oven</u>, as well as the <u>two sides and the floor under the stove.</u>
2. Stove vent hood and fan compartment will be thoroughly cleaned, if applicable. Occupants will remove and clean vent cover and walls of vent, but will not wash fan motor.
3. The refrigerator will be defrosted, cleaned, and wiped dry. <u>Do not use sharp objects to clear ice!</u> Ice and vegetable trays should be

returned to their place and <u>refrigerator door left in open position.</u> If it has wheels, pull out and clean floor.

4. Toilets, bathtubs, showers, cabinets, and all fixtures will be thoroughly cleaned.

5. Picture hooks and hangers will be removed from the walls. <u>All holes must be spackled and sanded.</u>

6. <u>Carpets will be steam cleaned.</u> Please leave receipt on the kitchen counter along with keys. Cigarette burns or other abuse of carpets will be subject to some loss of security deposit.

7. Kitchen cabinets will be cleaned and free from all grease, dirt, and shelf-covering. Doors closed; drawers shut. (Thumb tacks removed)

8. Hardwood and tile floors will be cleaned and waxed, if applicable.

9. Walls and ceilings that are soiled by grease, dirt, smears, etc. must be washed down. <u>Clean inside of windows; outside of windows, if accessible.</u>

10. Remove all cobwebs with a broom from the corners of all rooms, including closets.

11. Clean all ceiling fans and mini blinds, if applicable.

12. Use a damp cloth to wash off horizontal surfaces (window & door frames; baseboards along the floor).

13. Closets will be free of trash. Shelves and hanger rods will be cleaned.

14. Replace dead smoke alarm batteries. Clean light cover and replace old bulbs.

15. Storage rooms will be cleaned and all trash removed, if applicable.

16. Remove all wallpaper and/or borders including the adhesive, if applicable.

17. Garage, basement swept, and refuse removed from premises, if applicable.

18. Air conditioner filters must be cleaned, if applicable.

19. **<u>If you have gas, electric, or water taken out of your name, please notify Del Val Property! You can take out of your name, but do NOT have service turned off.</u>**

20. Arrangements with trash hauler must be made in advance for removal of large discarded items. An extra charge will be issued by the trash hauler.
21. <u>Leave all keys on kitchen counter.</u>

CHARGES UPON TERMINATION

If residence is not returned in the same condition as when rented, the following minimum charges will be deducted from the Security Deposit. The cost of labor and materials for cleaning, repairs, removals, and replacements, where applicable, of rent loss due to necessary repair time, and numerous other charges based on actual damages, will be deducted from the security deposit.

CLEANING not done by you:	MINIMUM CHARGES
Stove or oven	$75.00
Refrigerator	$55.00
Kitchen Sink	$20.00
Cabinets	$12.50 each
Countertops	$5.00
Floor (Kitchen)	$50.00
Toilet	$30.00
Shower/Tub	$75.00
Medicine Cabinet	$15.00
Vanity	$5.00
Floor (Bathroom)	$30.00
Trash Removal (per room)	$30.00
Windows	$15.00 per window
Bedroom Floors (vacuum)	$25.00 each room
Tile Cleaning	$25.00
Carpet Cleaning	$75.00/room, $45 hallway/stairs
Closets	$10.00 each
Extensive Cleaning (any room)	$100.00

DAMAGE:	
Negligent soiling or damage to walls	$250.00/room to paint
Removal or wall covering	$35.00 per hour
Nail holes or other small holes	$2.50 each
Larger holes (1/2"–2")	$5.00 each
Cigarette burns in carpeting	$95.00 each
Rugs/pads requiring replacement	$25.00 per square yd./ft.
Light bulb replacements	$5.00 each
Missing keys	$25.00
Lock replacement	$75.00 each, plus cost of locks
Lawn: trim shrubs, mow, and weed	$125.00 minimum
Missing screens	$50.00 each
Broken windows	$75.00 minimum each

LEASE RENEWAL ADDENDUM

ADDENDUM TO LEASE

This Addendum to Lease dated the [day] of [month], 2023. **Between** [Company or landlord name] AND [tenant's name].

Background

A) [Company or landlord name] (the "Landlord"), and [tenant's name] (the "Tenant") entered into a residential Lease (the "Lease") dated [Original lease date], 2023 for [property address and unit number].

B) The Landlord and Tenant desire to amend the Lease on the terms and conditions set forth in this Addendum to Lease (the "Agreement") by changing the following terms:

- Extending the lease one (1) year ending [date one year from current end date], 2023, with rent increasing to $xxx.xx per month.
- [Other changes you may want to make]

C) All other terms and conditions remain the same.

D) This is the [First or Second or Third] Amendment to the Lease.

IN CONSIDERATION OF the Landlord and Tenant agreeing to amend their obligations in the existing Lease, and other valuable consideration, the receipt and sufficiency of which is hereby acknowledged, and both Landlord and Tenant agree to keep, perform, and fulfill the promises, conditions, and agreements of the Lease dated [Original lease date], 2023.

_____   _____

[Owner or Landlord Name], Landlord   Date

_____   _____

[Tenant's Name], Tenant   Date

APPENDIX C

SAMPLE APPLICATION

```
┌──────────────────────────────────────────────┐
│ Del Val Realty & Property Management           │
└──────────────────────────────────────────────┘
```

RENTAL APPLICATION AND AUTHORIZATION TO RELEASE INFORMATION

Each occupant and co-applicant 18 years or older must submit a separate application

Submit this form **WITH A CASHIER'S CHECK OR MONEY ORDER** for a **non-refundable Application Fee** of $50.00 for the first applicant and $50 for each additional applicant and co-signer.

Once complete please mail with the Application Fee to **Del Val Realty & Property management, 49 E. Lancaster Avenue, Suite 300, Malvern, PA 19355.** You may also fax to **610-500-5682** and mail the original application with eh Application Fee to the above address. This form may be printed or typed. If you need help or have questions about this form please call our office at **484-328-3282.**

Address of Apartment Applying For:	Move-in date desired:
Name: (First) (Middle) (Last)	Any credit under other names?
Date of Birth:	D.L.#/State/Expiration:	Soc. Sec. #:
Home Phone: Work Phone:	Cellular Phone:
Email Address:	Alternate Email Address:

Proposed Occupants: List all others excluding yourself. Attach Additional Sheet if needed.	
Name: (First) (Middle) (Last)	Age:
Name: (First) (Middle) (Last)	Age:

PART I - RESIDENCE HISTORY (CURRENT & PREVIOUS 5 YEAR PERIOD)

Current Address:	Apt. #	Rent $:
(City) (State) (Zip)	Move in Date:	Move out Date:
Property Owner/Manager Name:	Manager's Phone	
Reason for Moving:		
Previous Address:	Apt. #:	Rent $:

THE RENTAL AGREEMENT WILL NOT BECOME EFFECTIVE UNTIL THIS APPLICATION IS APPROVED BY THE MANAGEMENT.

				Move in Date:	Move out Date:

(City)   (State)   (Zip)

Property Owner/Manager Name:	Manager's Phone:

Reason for Moving:

Previous Address:	Apt. #:	Rent $:

				Move in Date:	Move out Date:

(City)   (State)   (Zip)

Property Owner/Manager Name:	Manager's Phone:

Reason for Moving:

Have you ever been or are you now being evicted from a residence?	YES	NO

If yes, please explain:

Have you ever been convicted of any crime?	YES	NO

If yes, please explain:

Pets?	How many?	Type?	Do you smoke?	YES	NO

Personal Vehicle Info:

(Make)   (Model)   (Year)   (Plate #)

Incorporated/Company Vehicle Info:

(Make)   (Model)   (Year)   (Plate #)

PART II - EMPLOYMENT HISTORY (LAST TWO YEARS) & INCOME INFORMATION

Current Employer:	Title:	How long?	Mo. Income $
Address:	Supervisor:		Phone:

Previous Employer:	Title:	How long?	Mo. Income $
Address:	Supervisor:		Phone:

Other sources of additional income that are to be used to meet income requirements, please specify:

PART III – CREDIT

THE RENTAL AGREEMENT WILL NOT BECOME EFFECTIVE UNTIL THIS APPLICATION IS APPROVED BY THE MANAGEMENT

Revised 10/11   Page 2 of 3

Have you ever filed bankruptcy?	When?	Any Judgments/Collections Against You?
In case of Emergency, Notify:		Relationship:
Address:		Phone:
(Street)	(City)	(State) (Zip)

PART IV – AUTHORIZATION

The undersigned declares that the information on this Rental Application is true and correct, and understands that false statements may result in rejection of this and any future applications for housing which DEL VAL manages. The undersigned does further understand that all persons of firms named may freely give any requested information concerning the undersigned and hereby waives all right to action for any consequences resulting from such information. My signature below authorizes investigation of all statements contained herein by the management company, including but not limited to a credit check. I further understand and agree that DEL VAL will rely upon this Rental Application as an inducement for entering into a rental agreement or lease and I warrant that the facts contained in this Application are true. If any facts are proven to be untrue, DEL VAL may terminate my tenancy immediately and collect any damages incurred, including reasonable attorneys fees resulting therefrom. All or part of the above information may be made available to other screening and collection services. Pursuant to Pennsylvania Law, you are also herein notified that a negative credit report reflecting on your credit record may be submitted in the future to a credit reporting agency if you fail to fulfill the terms of your rental obligations or if you default in those obligations in any way. DEL VAL welcomes all applicants. It is illegal and against our policy to discriminate against any person because of race, color, religion, sex, sexual orientation, national origin, mental or physical disability, or familial status.

Applicants Signature:_____ Date:_____

Email Address _____

PART V – CONSUMER NOTICE

CONSUMER NOTICE- THIS IS NOT A CONTRACT

_____ hereby states that with respect to this property, I am acting in the following capacity:
(Check one)
    owner/landlord of the property;
    a direct employee of the owner/landlord;
    an agent of the owner/landlord pursuant to a property management or exclusive listing agreement.

I acknowledge that I have received this notice:

_____   _____
(Consumer)   (Date)

I certify that I have provided this notice:

_____   _____
(Licensee)   (Date)

THE RENTAL AGREEMENT WILL NOT BECOME EFFECTIVE UNTIL THIS APPLICATION IS APPROVED BY THE MANAGEMENT

APPENDIX D

WELCOME LETTER

[Date], 2024

ELECTRONIC AND REGULAR MAIL

[Tenant's name and address]

Dear [tenant's first name]:

Welcome to your new rental property! I [Owner or landlord name] would like to take this opportunity to extend a warm welcome to you and let you know just what you can expect from us in the future. We have listed some items below that will address any questions you may have concerning your new rental property.

Contact Info... You may have questions regarding different aspects of your tenancy. The following is contact information for various issues.

- Maintenance calls: [provide details of how to make maintenance requests]
- Bookkeeping issues: [provide details of who and where to call with bookkeeping questions]

Paying Rent Online Electronically... You will receive an email invitation from our Property Management Software called [software name]. Once you open the email, there will be a link and instructions on how to log on to the [software name] site and set up your own password.

[provide details on how they will pay rent electronically]

Utilities Concierge: We offer a utility concierge service to assist you in setting up your utilities including electric, gas, and water plus any phone, cable, or security needs. To sign up for the utility concierge, please go to [website]. (If you do not offer this service delete this section.)

Renter's Insurance ... One of the requirements of your lease is to have renter's insurance. You can obtain this through your own insurance agent and send us proof of insurance and adding [landlord name] as an Additional Interest. If you do not have an insurance agent, we work with an insurance broker that specializes in this type of renter's insurance. You can contact our insurance broker at [enter phone number]. Renter's insurance can be set up over the phone for a very modest monthly fee.

Maintenance ... As we expect you to pay your rent promptly, you can expect us to respond promptly to maintenance problems. ALL maintenance requests must be sent through our software [software name]. If you need assistance with the system the first time you put in a maintenance request, please call us at [phone number] during our normal business hours (Monday–Friday, 8:00–4:30).

You must maintain the interior and exterior of your home. For the exterior, this includes keeping trash off the lawn or backyard and keeping the exterior of the property in a neat and tidy manner.

In the interior, if appropriate, we expect you to change furnace filters every three months, change smoke alarm batteries twice a year, and complete minor repairs including small leaks, faucet repairs, and keeping items from clogging toilets. Please note, if appropriate, the following repairs will be charged to you including:

- Clogged sinks—from food that should have been placed in trash.
- Clogged toilets—from flushing items other than human waste (feminine hygiene products, toys, excess paper, clothing, or cleaning products).
- Leaks—from shoving items under sink (this knocks water and drain lines loose).

- Faucet knobs—from using too much force, causing broken knobs and leaving faucets.
- that leak unresolved.
- Broken items—broken windows, doors, glass, or locks for any reason.
- Storm doors—storm doors if not properly closed.

Please complete the enclosed Tenant Information Sheet.

Move-In Checklist... Please be reminded that Tenants are required to fill in Move-in Checklist (included with your Lease) and send to [your office] within seven (7) days of the move-in date. If the Checklist is not received within that time, [Landlord] considers The Leased Unit was accepted as satisfactory by Tenant. The Checklist can be mailed to our office as listed on Page 1 or faxed to [fax number].

We believe that communication, cooperation, and respect is a two-way street and the key to an excellent working relationship.

_____

[Signature]

ABOUT THE AUTHOR

MIKE LAUTENSACK left a nearly two-decade career in the corporate finance world to become a full-time real estate investor in 2006. The following year, he founded Del Val Realty & Property Management, a full-service residential property management company based in Philadelphia. Today, Del Val serves over 550 clients with over 5,500 single-family, multifamily, and HOA units under management. Over these past sixteen years, Mike has managed over 7,500 rental units, signed over 4,000 leases, collected over $50 million in rent, and has become a leader in the property management field.